Well Preserved
A Jam-Making Hymnal

Joan Hassol

ILLUSTRATIONS BY A. R. SHAPIRO

A FIRESIDE BOOK
Published by Simon & Schuster

For my six children and their families, whose love, support and encouragement have sustained me beyond measure the past six years

FIRESIDE
Rockefeller Center
1230 Avenue of the Americas
New York, NY 10020

Designed by Deborah Kerner

Manufactured in the United States of America

10 9 8 7 6 5 4 3 2 1

Library of Congress Cataloging-in-Publication Data
Hassol, Joan.
    Well preserved: a jam-making hymnal/Joan Hassol;
illustrations by A. R. Shapiro.
      p. cm.
      "A Fireside Book."
      Includes index.
      1. Jam.
  TX612.J3H37   1998
  641.8'52—dc21   98-11177   CIP
ISBN 0-684-83921-0

Grateful acknowledgment is made for permission to reprint the following:
"Turning Toward the Morning" by Gordon Bok. Used by permission of Folk-Legacy
Records, Sharon, CT.

Acknowledgments

LIFE IS FULL of unexpected and inexplicable events that, in hindsight, seem predestined, not to be questioned. When Meg Ruley called me the first time, after reading a proposal for another book, and told me that she had been one of my husband's students, I knew that I was about to embark on a wonderful journey. I have not been disappointed. She has been joyful with and for me; supportive and kind; understanding that, as a first-time solo author, I would need more than just a little hand-holding. And she found Sarah Baker! Sarah made the whole process of writing and rewriting a delight instead of a chore. Her unbounded enthusiasm has been contagious, her support constant. My world has expanded, my family enhanced. What more could any author want?

To all my friends, who have listened to me talk endlessly about this project, my thanks. All of you have made the painful process of starting over and moving on so much easier. I am a very lucky woman.

*

Contents

Winter

Spring

Summer

Breads, Muffins and Other Delectables

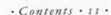

Preface

I DON'T REMEMBER not being able to make jam. It's like learning to ride a bike. One day you can't, the next you can. So it was with jam.

I have always been a hunter-gatherer. I remember when I was five years old being taught by my cousin Banice how to find quahogs with my toes in the sand flats in Rhode Island. The excitement of discovery is still with me.

The concept for *Well Preserved* arose from my feelings while searching for, picking and preserving wild fruit, and finally storing hundreds of jars of jam. I'm deeply connected to that process. For each season there is a rhythm; for each season a particular smell; for each season the "just right time" to be in the woods or fields.

There is something about finding the succulent, almost ripe fruits; about picking berries; about laboring in the hot sun, that awakens long-dormant memories of a sun-washed early childhood. I'm still a hunter-gatherer, with an instinctive sense of needing to "have enough." Turning fruits and berries into jam continues to fill that primordial need to find my own food. The experience is one of peace. Making jam is my meditation, stirring jam in bubbling pots my serenity. Stacking jars fills me with a sense of security. Jam making is an intuitive, almost joyful connection between the fruit and me. It's a sensual, earth-related, personal expression of what it *feels* like to make jam. I'm aware that my relationship with the earth and what I experience as my life's journey are deeply intertwined.

In 1990, I decided to turn what had been a once-in-a-while lark when beach plums were ripe into a business. Living on Cape Cod, I knew that tourists would buy a locally produced, natural product. Well Preserved was born with a logo designed by my husband, Len, who, at the time, was terminally ill with cancer. It was to be his last gift. I am reminded of him every time I put a label on a jar.

At the same time I started making jam, I opened up my bed-and-breakfast. My guests have been my best critics. They do not hesitate to tell me which jams they like the best, which ones need more zip and which are too runny. And what better remembrance of a nice time than a jar of homemade jam to take with you!

The first summer of the jam business was not a rousing success. I just about broke even. Len remarked, "Smucker's is not beating a path to your door," but I was satisfied. The terror of his illness and his imminent death was made easier when I made jam.

I hadn't expected to have to learn how to walk on the hot coals of grief. I hadn't expected to have the computer that runs in my head sorting out all the things that one has to manage when one is alone rule my waking moments. I hadn't expected to have my body shriek with the need to be held, to be touched, to be cherished.

I met Len when I was very young—nineteen years old. I was a student nurse and a cellist in a community orchestra (I am still an active cellist). He was a postgraduate student, worldwise, from New York and very handsome. We met at an inn near Tanglewood, the summer home of the Boston Symphony. In an attempt to keep me in nursing school and to assuage my feelings of resentment at not being able to go to music school, my father financed a week at Tanglewood for me. The romance was quick and intense. After four dates, over a period of ten months, we were married, and embarked on a remarkable, complex, lusty thirty-seven years.

I now think that Len was bemused by me. A quiet, intellectual therapist and professor, he was, at times, overwhelmed by our rambunctious, fast-growing family. We ended up with six children—four biological and two adopted. Little did he know when he left Brooklyn that he would embark on a life of endless diapers, litters of dogs and cats, carnivals in the front yard or trips to rescue stranded children in remote mountain locations. There was never a dull moment.

I had expected that after many years of working hard, both professionally and at home, and of raising our children, he and I would take to the seas, visit far-off places only alluded to in the travel section of *The New York Times;* dig clams when we wanted to; find oysters at low tide, ready to eat with a flick of the knife; fish the incoming tides for striped bass; volunteer our time and energy to a knee-high list of worthy causes; in short, retire in the manner prescribed in all those books on "getting older."

Instead, neatly labeled jars of jam became my reality. Oh, I still play the cello a lot; I still volunteer more than I should for all those worthy causes; I do some traveling; I garden intensely and I still have lots of energy left over.

The reality is that life frequently feels disconnected. Even today, seven years later, jam making centers me. Lining jam jars up in orderly rows centers me. It is still my most palpable reality. When all else seems unreal, when loneliness and anguish flood my spirit, when sleep eludes me, I make jam.

I am also a musician. I've been able to read music as long as I've been able to read. First grade and music lessons started together. The combination of jam and music was inevitable. The jam pots come out, the fruit is assembled, the counters and tools sanitized, the music chosen. If I am ill at ease and troubled, one kind of music; if peaceful, another. My body heaves an audible sigh of relief when the music starts and the pot boils.

What started small has grown into a "just the right size" business—small enough for me to manage myself; large enough to provide a small income. This year I will sell approximately five thousand jars. I have an inspected, approved kitchen, several local outlets, loyal customers and, most of all, a wonderful way of dealing with life's stresses.

This book is about my relationship with jam, my soul, music and the world in which I live. The recipes are some that have evolved over the years. Some are traditional, others pure inventions. Jam making has become my meditational exercise. When I make jam I slow down, my actions become rhythmical, my thinking clear. The repetitive motions of washing, stirring, pouring and labeling allow me the space to think about my life— what it means to be starting over and how I can embrace this stage of my life with vitality and joy.

✳

Introduction

JAM MAKING is not mysterious work. Simple in concept, ingredients and tools, it is a delightful way to enjoy the bountiful gifts of the harvest—freshly picked strawberries, boxes of sweet-smelling apricots and peaches, beach plums ripening on secret bushes, grapes hanging in abundant clusters. All await my attention. During the summer months when I'm under pressure to produce, I try to visualize snowy winter evenings, snug by my woodstove, enjoying hot bran muffins or Irish soda bread, amply spread with some wonderful jam like rhubarb or tangy marmalade.

Friends call asking me to join them for dinner. "Oh, by the way, I'm all out of jam," says Mary. She laughs as she wonders if it's my company or my jam that's more important. I *always* have enough for friends. You can, too!

Fruit

The real joy in jam making is finding the fruit. I feel like a detective watching the supermarket ads, looking for the notice that announces the opening of a picking farm, checking in with my "sources," revisiting all my berry spots. The search gets me outside, tramping over the moors and fields. My children call to invite me to go picking apples and pears in the fall. My friends call to tell me when their grapes are ripe.

Sometimes I'm blessed with unexpected largess on the part of a merchant. This year Meredith, who owns the farm store that was the first to carry my jam, called to tell me that they would be closing for a few months during the winter and were cleaning out the freezer. "Could you use a few boxes of frozen raspberries?" A "few" boxes turned out to be close to a hundred pounds of frozen berries. I popped them into my freezers, promising Meredith that I'd repay her in jam when she reopens. Her son, who operates a wholesale fruit business, gets me fruit at the wholesale market. I've discovered that people are willing and pleased to help if I tell them what I'm doing. Even the clerks at the supermarket know that I make jam and are not surprised when I come to the checkout with sixty-four bags of sugar on a cart!

Sometimes, fruit travels many miles to reach me. My son Roger brings Maine blueberries. Other neighbors arrive very late at night with boxes of blueberries, having driven for hours from Maine. I buy frozen fruit when fresh fruit is either out of season or not plentiful enough. Quiescent, or individually frozen, berries are sometimes superior to fresh fruit and can be significantly cheaper. The best source of frozen fruit in larger quantities is hotel and restaurant supply vendors. When I buy berries this way, I separate the berries into smaller bags and store them in the freezer. Some fruit, like cranberries, are abundant during the fall harvest but can be in short supply by the end of the summer. When I can't find enough to pick myself, I buy them already sliced and frozen.

I feel like the ant in the parable of the ant and the grasshopper—assured I'll have enough fruit to last all winter. Then when I go to the freezer, I can pick and choose which jam to make; I can savor the smells and bring back memories of warm sun and family gatherings.

Pectin

Webster's defines pectin as "a white amorphous carbohydrate occurring in ripe fruits, with the ability to solidify to a gel." Pectin is what makes jam jell.

All fruits contain pectin, some more than others. Fruit that is not fully ripe contains more pectin than fruit that is overly ripe. Make sure that 25 percent of the fruit you use in each recipe is not fully ripe.

Some jam makers prepare their own pectin stock from apple juice concentrate, or do not use pectin at all, preferring to boil the fruit and sugar until it's just right. I use commercial powdered pectin in my jam recipes. Similar to pectin you buy in the market, I buy my pectin in 50-pound boxes, enough to make 2,500 jars. I pay attention to the natural pectin content of the fruit I'm working with and try to combine fruits with low pectin content with fruit containing more pectin. Then I'm assured of a good gel. Well, most of the time. There are those days when the jam gods are frowning and nothing seems to work. I've discovered that high humidity can wreak havoc in the kitchen. The jam sometimes just doesn't want to jell. When that happens I unscrew the caps, empty the jam back into the pot, add a little sugar and a little lemon juice and try again. I do not add more pectin. If, after a second try, I still have sauce instead of jam, I smile and label the jars Pancake Sauce, a wonderful hostess gift. With careful measuring and experience, you too can use pectin to make jam that is not rubbery, has

no aftertaste and takes infinitely less time to make. Just remember, always sterilize your jars and use new caps if you have to try twice.

Sugar

Use granulated sugar. After trial and error I've learned to buy sugar in 5- or 10-pound bags. I can lift those. Since sugar tends to absorb moisture and can get as hard as concrete, I store my sugar in sealed boxes in my furnace room. I keep a dehumidifier going all summer. In the winter when the furnace is on, I don't have a moisture problem.

Jars

When I started making jam, I was offered crates and crates of old jars—ones with glass covers, ones with two-piece covers. I reluctantly turned down all of them. I use modern jars. They have a one-piece cap with a plastic seal built into the underside. These jars are easy to sterilize and handle, and seal well with no paraffin. Jam jars and lids are available in small quantities in most supermarkets and hardware stores during the fall season.

I get my jars by the truckload, thousands and thousands at a time. For a while they were coming in an 18-wheeler down my narrow road. I shudder to think what the neighbors thought was going on in my house! I've since found some wonderful people who bring my jars in their pickup truck, a little quieter for the neighbors.

Tools

Jam-making tools are simplicity personified. Everything you need is easy to find and readily available. I'll list what I use and find handy. Here's what you need:

Eight-Quart Stainless Steel Pots

Pots need to be deep and widemouthed so that the jam won't boil over or splatter. Stainless steel is nonreactive.

Nonslotted Stainless Steel Spoons

I recommend long-handled commercial-grade spoons so that you are kept out of reach of bubbling, boiling jam. The jam flows off them just the right way to evaluate sheeting.

Two-Quart Stainless Steel or Plastic Measuring Containers

I've found narrow ones with narrow lips much easier to use than the traditional widemouthed measuring cup. They are usually available at restaurant supply stores.

Food Processor

A food processor is indispensable. Into it goes many kinds of fruit—citrus fruit with the peels on, cranberries, rhubarb, peaches, pears. Don't puree the fruit. Use the pulse button to control the texture of the fruit.

Zesters, Strippers and Peelers

I promise, this is not a vaudeville routine. These tools are great for removing the peel from citrus fruits. The zester takes off narrow slivers of peel, leaving behind the bitter pith, which you don't want in some recipes. The stripper takes off a little larger strip of peel and the peeler a still larger strip.

Cheesecloth

Cheesecloth is used to wrap spices in little envelopes of exotic flavors, especially in chutney recipes. Wash the cheesecloth before using to get rid of the sizing or stiffening that's put in at the time of manufacture.

Flat Sieve

While not essential, this is a useful tool to skim off the foam on the top of the pot before pouring the jam into jars. Foam is unsightly and forms a thick scum when it jells, so it's better to remove it.

Thermometer

Some people feel more comfortable using a thermometer to indicate when the jam is ready to pour. If you want to use a thermometer, buy one that's used for candy making.

Tongs

Tongs are used to lift jars and covers out of hot water.

Foley Food Mill

When I want to make seedless jam, I cook the fruit briefly and then put it through the food mill. The skins and seeds or pits are left behind. I then make jam with the puree and juice.

Fruit Preparation

Preparing the fruit for jam making is the most important and time-consuming part of the operation. When I bring fruit such as peaches, pears or apricots home, I handle them with a very soft touch. They are stored in a single layer in a big box, and when just slightly soft to the touch I go to work. After washing pears or apricots, for example, I core and slice them up and put them in my food processor *unpeeled*. A few seconds of chopping, not pureeing, and the fruit is ready to put into zip-lock bags and store in the freezer. Pear and apricot skins are tight. The additional roughness of the chopped skin provides a nice texture. This chopping technique is also useful for rhubarb.

Peaches are blanched by cooking in a deep pot, so the peaches are covered with water. After bringing the water to a boil, I turn off the heat and monitor the peaches. In a few minutes the skins begin to slip. At that point I put the peaches into a sink filled with ice cold water and, presto, the skins come right off. The peaches are ready to have the pits removed, chopped up and stored in zip-lock bags in the freezer.

I freeze blueberries unwashed. If you wash them first, the water freezes on them and the cells of the fruit break down. I also chop up blueberries, but do it when they are still partially frozen, when I am about to use them. I've found that chopping fruit like blueberries and strawberries guarantees well-distributed fruit in each jar. There is nothing more frustrating than to pour jam into jars and have all the fruit on the top. The first few jars end up with all the fruit!

I pick strawberries at a local farm and then watch the market prices carefully, buying when the prices are down. I chop them up before freezing and put just a quart in each zip-lock bag, making storage much easier. Quiescent, individually frozen, unsweetened strawberries also make good jam.

Jar Preparation and Sealing

Clean tools, sterile jars and caps and very clean work surfaces all add up to a pure end product.

Only jars manufactured for home use should be used. These tend to be sturdier than some others used for commercial products such as syrup or salad dressings. Since very large jars are very difficult to seal properly, use only jars that hold either 4 or 8 ounces. All the recipes in this book call for 8-ounce jars.

Jars available for home use have covers that can be replaced easily. Never use covers more than once. The plastic ring inside the one-piece cover gets compressed when screwed onto the jar and cannot provide the needed seal if used again.

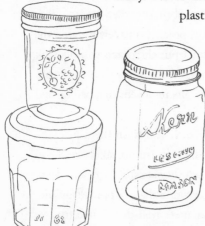

Wash jars in hot, soapy water. Rinse well. Place jars on a rack in a kettle. Fill the kettle until the jars are submerged. Bring the water to a boil and boil for 15 minutes. Leave the jars in the hot water, taking the jars out individually as you fill them.

Wash the one-piece covers in hot, soapy water. Place in a large kettle. Cover with water. Bring the water to a boil and boil for 5 minutes. Take out covers as you need them.

If you intend to use jars that use two-part covers, wash the jars as just indicated. Wash the covers with hot, soapy water and boil as indicated by the manufacturer, generally 15 minutes. Do not boil rubber inner jar rings. Pour boiling water over these inner rings and let them sit in the hot water until you need them.

You can, of course, use jars over and over. You can reuse the outer screwbands of the two-part covers. Never use the lid itself again. Always check jar edges and screwbands to make sure they are not chipped, rusted or bent.

I do not use paraffin. It is difficult to work with, and many people do not like to have petroleum products on their food. I fill each jar, leaving ⅛ inch at the top of the jar; make sure the rim is clean, cap and invert (turn upside down) immediately, placing the jar on a clean counter. A vacuum is set up, sealing the jar. This technique is effective and safe only if the jars, the jam and the covers are boiling hot.

When you invert the jar, the hot contents of the jar are held against the cover, sealing the jar. I set the jars upright in 5 minutes, leave on a rack to cool overnight and store in a cool place.

The Cooking Process

I make jam in small batches. Each recipe makes approximately 7 or 8 jars. Some will make more, depending on the size of the fruit used. Chutney recipes may make as many as 10 to 12 jars.

Working in small batches allows you to control the process and be creative, try new combinations, and have enough variety to satisfy friends and family. Who wants a shelf full of only grape jam!

Now, you've washed your jars and lids, your fruit is ready, your sugar measured, your pectin set. The alchemy starts! I generally put 2 tablespoons of bottled reconstituted lemon juice in all my recipes. The exception will be marmalades, which do not need the additional citrus acid. The acid in lemon juice enhances the action of the pectin and helps set up the fruit, besides adding a lovely tang to the finished product.

Into the pot goes the fruit. I generally use 1 quart of fruit per recipe. There are exceptions, which will be indicated in the recipes. Some recipes call for the fruit to be simmered for a few minutes as part of the process, and some, like chutney, require much longer cooking and monitoring.

I put the fruit and lemon juice in all at once. I then bring the pot to a boil. When the fruit comes to the boil, I add the pectin. When the pot comes to the boil again, I slowly add the sugar, stirring constantly to prevent the fruit from scorching and to know when it is ready to pour. I've found that timing my cooking or using a thermometer doesn't help. I have to feel the jam, watch the color and consistency change, and feel the jam move in just the right way. Jam changes color just before it's ready to pour. All the cloudiness leaves, the bubbles become smaller and the jam becomes almost translucent. When ready, the spoon moves a little more slowly through the jam, not sticking, but with a little more resistance. At the same time I let spoonfuls of jam drop off my spoon. When perfect, jam needs to "sheet" off the spoon, not drip. Instead of single droplets, the jam flows off the spoon. Sometimes, as it flows off, thick drops form. Then it is ready.

*

Marmalades are best tested by using the cold plate method. Put a flat plate in the refrigerator to get chilled. When you're ready, put a teaspoonful of hot marmalade on the plate. Leave the plate in the refrigerator for about 10 minutes. If a skin develops, the marmalade is ready to pour. If not, continue cooking and stirring, and try again in a few minutes. Because you do not add any pectin to most marmalade recipes, it is important to monitor the jelling process. Don't get discouraged if, after you pour your jam or marmalade, it does not set for 24 hours or so. The Zen admonition of just letting go is good advice here. Whatever is will be!

Some people do not like seeds in their jam. In that case, I cook the fruit with a little water for a few moments, primarily to make it easier to work with, put it through a Foley Food Mill and then process as usual. This technique is useful when preparing fruit like beach plums, wild cherries or grapes. The end product is a thick juice, which I then pour into 1-quart plastic containers and freeze, remembering to allow room for expansion at the top. There's nothing worse than going into the freezer and discovering frozen juice everywhere.

When you make chutney, you must process the filled jars in a boiling water bath. This process assures a well-sealed, well-cooked product, with no chance of any contamination. The boiling water bath is used only for those foods that have a high-acid content, such as pickles, relishes and chutney. Other foods with a low-acid content must be canned in a pressure canner. The process for chutney is as follows:

* Buy a canning pot that has a rack in it. The pot needs to be deep enough so there will be room for 2 inches of water over

the top of the jars and enough additional room for the bubbling of the boiling water.

* Put the canning pot on the stove and fill halfway with water. Turn on the stove and start heating the water.

* Fill a teakettle with water and start that heating up.

* Fill the hot, sterilized jars (see section on jar preparation, pages 24–25) with boiling chutney. Screw the covers on securely, but not extremely tightly.

* Stand the jars on the rack in the canning pot. The number of jars you can process at one time depends on the size of the jar. Jars must not touch. The water has to circulate around the jars.

* Pour enough additional hot water around the jars so that there are 2 inches of water above the top of the jars.

* Bring the canning pot to a boil and boil for 10 minutes.

* Remove the jars from the canning pot with tongs. Make sure the covers are tightened securely. Place on a rack to cool. Store in a cool, dark place.

Spices and Flavorings

Be creative! Take a chance. Try out new combinations, flavors and additions. I use liqueurs, intense oils and spices. I try exotic combinations, which I will share with you. I use a lot of preserved ginger. My chutney calls for cardamom pods, stick cinnamon, cloves and allspice. I feel like one of the three kings as I mix and match. Like the sorcerer's apprentice, I wave the magic wand of far-off places to create a wondrous palate of tastes. Because spices and liqueurs contain volatile oils, which lose their flavors if overheated, I add them at the end of the cooking process.

Storing Jam

After making, let the jam rest overnight on a rack. Then store in a cool, dry place out of the sun. A cool cellar is ideal. Check to make sure no mold has started to grow, and discard any jam that does develop it.

When the temperature dips to minus 10 degrees and the wind howls, how satisfying it is to go downstairs to my cellar, turn on the light and survey those jars—amber, claret, ruby red, golden yellow, pale green. Each one holds the promise of delightful tastes and memories of warm summer days.

✳

Fall

PURE
PRESERVE
FRUIT

October First

I WAKE EARLY, generally around 4:30 A.M. It's called the hour of the owl. By five-thirty, the dog, a little bichon frise incongruously named Monster, and I are out walking on the bike path. It's our early morning ritual. She sniffs all the smells left overnight by raccoons, skunks and an occasional deer. I meditate as I walk. My friend Ed, a Buddhist, says that you do not have to sit cross-legged and uncomfortable on the floor to meditate. Meditation, he says, can be active. I just have to learn to acknowledge what is happening—to observe it, and let it go. It takes a few miles to awaken my soul, to clear my head, to hear my breathing. A few miles to become acutely aware of each step I take. It's easy to just *be* out here. No need to even think about control.

Today I heard a rooster crowing. "Ah. He's the conductor." I knew I would soon hear the rest of the orchestra warming up. Tufted titmice, cardinals, chickadees, robins, blue jays and nuthatches join in. Woodpeckers are the snare drums; flickers, the timpani. Looking up, I can see the bare branches of the locust trees, killed but not top-pled in the raging hurricane of 1991. Clinging to the sides of the trees is the audience. Dozens of birds. Waiting for the warmth of the sun, they position themselves to be directly in the path of the rising sun's rays. I turn my head. I, too, want to catch the first warmth of the sun.

This time of year the woods have a distinct smell.

Slightly sweet, slightly pungent, it is the smell of decay, of over-ripeness. The smells rise up as I scuff my feet through the leaves.

" 'Come little leaves,' said the wind one day. 'Come over the meadow with me and play. Put on your dresses of red and gold, for summer is gone and the days grow cold.' " I find myself humming an old childhood song as I tramp along. The smell gets stronger and stronger as I kick over more and more leaves. The decay of rebirth. It's from the oak leaves. Oak trees are the predominant deciduous trees on the outer Cape. The leaves are full of tannic acid. When they drop and rot, they smell. The smell is a reminder that it's time to look for wild Concord grapes. I can smell them as I walk. The grapevines are all over the tree trunks. They crowd out other plants. They creep and crawl over bushes, and like most plants, bloom and fruit up where the sun reaches them. I can see grapes. I can smell them. They lie splattered on the ground. Most of them are beyond my grasp.

I can go where they are easy to pick. Friends call to ask if I'd like to harvest their grapes. One grape arbor is close to the marsh where I used to live. The sea grass waving at the edge of the marsh has turned. Once a bright green, the long arching blades, like luxurious hair, wave tawny and golden.

Walking along the marsh after I've finished picking, I realize the color of the sky has changed. Not so obvious away from the immediate coast, once there I can see it. One day it's blue. The next day it's *blue!* Bright blue. Startlingly blue. Breath-catching blue. Blue that reflects in the water along the marsh. I've walked around the point at the edge of this marsh for almost forty years. I know every rivulet where water flows in and out with the tides. I know just where the sand turns into black, smelly, foot-sucking ooze, that wonderful stuff from whence all sea life comes. Here is where the newly hatched fish fry feed the fingerlings. They, in turn, become food for larger fish and on it goes, up the food chain. Marshes are the most vulnerable, valuable and delicate part of the Cape—the nursery for the entire fishing industry.

It's possible to walk across the flats to the other side at low tide. If I look closely, I can spot the holes where razor clams and quahogs are dug in. I've dug bushels of shellfish here. I've moored sailboats here. I've scattered treasured ashes here. Picking grapes surrounded by such beauty is not a chore. It's a blessing.

This year a friend told me about another grape arbor. I called the owner and, with her approval, went to pick grapes. This house isn't on the marsh. It's on a large pond. Ringing the pond shore are tupelo trees—trees that do well near water, trees that can stand to have their feet wet. Tupelo trees reward us with the most startling red leaves in the fall. On calm, windless days, the trees are reflected in the water. Monet couldn't hold a candle to tupelo trees in full autumn regalia.

Walking along the pond shore, I spy fox dens. Foxes, like most animals, including humans, I suppose, need to have two doors—one to get in and, in an emergency, one to get out. The entrances/exits are far enough apart, dug into the sloping ground around the shore, to give the foxes ample time to elude any predator. I've seen baby and adolescent foxes. It's reassuring to know that in this overdeveloped, overpaved, overregulated world, foxes still nest nearby, hunting for crayfish along the pond edge, watching for mice in the fields.

I pick my five-gallon bucket full of grapes. When I get home, I take off the stems, wash the grapes, put them in a large pot, cover them with water and simmer them until they are soft. I put them through the Foley Food Mill. The skins and seeds are left behind and I have beautiful, deep purple grape pulp. Some I make into jam immediately. Some I pour into quart bottles and freeze. Then some wild, wintry day, I can re-create October.

Not too many people buy wild grape jam. Perhaps they are reminded of too many peanut butter and jelly sandwiches from their youth. This grape jam is not your ordinary store-bought grape jam. This thick, tangy, sweet jam is filled with October. Regal, heart-stopping October. When I make grape jam, the house is filled with October.

✴

Concord Grape Jam

Dark purple, not too sweet, with a little bite, distinguishes wild grape jam from its supermarket competition. It tastes wonderful with peanut butter, or alone on plain toast.

4 cups grape pulp and juice
2 tablespoons lemon juice
1½ packages powdered pectin
7 cups sugar

Put the grape pulp and lemon juice in a large nonreactive pot. Bring to a boil. Add the pectin. Return to the boil. Add the sugar slowly, stirring constantly. Bring to the boil again and boil for 1 minute, or until the jam sheets off the spoon. Pour into hot, sterilized jars. Cover with new, clean, hot caps. (See section in introduction on jar and cover preparation, pages 24–25.) Invert for 5 minutes.

Makes 7–8 eight-ounce jars

Apple Grape Jam

3 cups grape pulp and juice
2 cups unsweetened applesauce
2 tablespoons lemon juice
1 ½ packages powdered pectin
9 cups sugar

Put the grape pulp, applesauce and lemon juice in a large nonre-active pot. Bring to a boil. Add the pectin. Return to the boil. Add the sugar slowly, stirring constantly. Bring to the boil again and boil for 1 minute, or until the jam sheets off the spoon. Pour into hot, sterilized jars. Cover with new, clean, hot caps. (See section in introduction on jar and cover preparation, pages 24–25.) Invert for 5 minutes.

Makes 8–9 eight-ounce jars

Chasing the Wild Cranberry

PROVINCETOWN, MASSACHUSETTS, is at the end of the world. Sticking out like a beckoning arm, pummeled by nor'easters in the winter and tourists in the summer, it is a very special place. For generations, the fishing industry held the town together. There are fewer fishing boats now, but the people whose families have been here for generations are sturdy.

P'Town, as it is affectionately called, is the place where artists and writers come to work; where independent nonconformists find a haven; where whales frolic in the inner harbor; you can eat some of the best food on the Cape and immerse yourself in some of the most spectacular landscapes. In the winter, the sand dunes flow up and over the one road leading to town. The snowplows plow sand, and a walk on the beach can literally be a breathtaking experience. The wind cleans out your circulation and your body is filled to the brim with wild new air from around the world.

Sometimes I drive to Provincetown when I have a need for real change in my rhythm—a need to clear my head, renourish my soul and change the air I breathe. I don't head for the center of town. I head for the Provincelands. With undulating sand dunes and wind-whipped stunted pine and oak trees, walking in the Provincelands is like walking on another planet. It is a place where a small flower in bloom seems a miracle and where seeing many flowers blooming in the spring, on tiny ground-hugging plants, is like peeking in on a fairy landscape. For it is here, in the Provincelands, that I come to pick wild cranberries.

Today, people tend to think of huge cranberry bogs, Ocean Spray cranberry collectives, mechanized machinery: big business. And so it is on the Cape. But long ago, Indians picked cranberries in the Provincelands. Where the national seashore guides take people in the fall to see what a cranberry bush looks like, Indians picked. I pick.

Cranberry bushes are tiny, delicate, evergreen plants. In the spring, the plants, which grow only a few inches high, are covered with little white flowers tinged with pink. Wedding bouquets for elves and fairies. If the winter has been wet, if the spring rains ample, if the bees arrive to pollinate, if the blossoms do not drop off before they are pollinated, if it stays damp through the early fall, then I find cranberries.

In October, when the air is just beginning to crisp around the edges and you need a jacket in the early morning, it's time to drive up to the Provincelands. I park by the side of the road, walk down an embankment and head out into the bogs. Once there were acres and acres of bogs. Over time other plants have intruded and the bogs have shrunken. Still there is plenty for me. If it's been a good year, with plenty of rain to keep the ground damp all summer and fall, there will be berries. Lots of berries. If the fairies had wedding bouquets in the spring, they have Christmas trees now. The bushes are loaded with miniature ornaments. Edible ornaments. Some are yellowish . . . not ripe. Some are pinkish . . . almost ripe. And some are ruby red. They are not uniform in size like the ones we get in a plastic bag. Finding a bush with big berries is a special treat, one to sing out about.

Picking is very hard work. The early settlers designed a scoop to pick cranberries with. My friend Marty made us one, looking like a hand-held comb with a small bucket attached. You bend over and pass the "comb" through the bush, being very careful not to break the branches. The berries fall into the scoop part and then can be emptied into a larger pail. Without a scoop, you can use your fingers like a comb. It takes a lot of cranberries to fill a bucket! It takes a lot of children picking to have enough to freeze! It takes keen eyesight to see all the berries hiding close to the ground. When you get right down among the plants you can see that you are not the only one who has been there. Deer and rabbit droppings are all around. If you listen very closely, and keep very still, you can hear the little folk. It's true. I leave some for them.

There is always competition for the berries. People tend to covet special spots and are reluctant to divulge where the *best* ones are. I understand. Finding a good crop of cranberries is one of the rare wonders of living at the end of the world. I told my friend Philip about the bogs. He told me about the cranberries that grow in the sand. Right in the dunes. I went there one year. Dune walking is very good exercise. It's nicer to say that than to say it's not fun and not easy. Oh, in the beginning I feel as if I'm setting off to find an oasis. That fantasy dies quickly, and all I can think of is how far I'll have to walk to get the berries and how far I'll have to walk back. But once started, it's impossible not to go on. Just the thought of a mother lode of cranberries is enough to keep me trudging on.

There is an oasis of sorts out there in the dunes. Surrounded by nothing but sand for as far as I can see is a round, damp place. And it's full of cranberry bushes! I've filled an old pillowcase with berries, slung the case over my shoulder and, like Saint Nick, made my way back to the road.

I handle those hard-won berries as if they were crown jewels. I have infinite respect for those first settlers who had to forage to survive. I pick because it makes me feel good. Berries are not elemental to my physical survival. Picking cranberries is essential to my soul's survival.

Nowadays, I need to buy cranberries by the boxful. I can't depend on the bees, the rains and the fairies for all my berries. It's a mixed blessing. I pick to stay connected to the bogs. And oh, how those jars of jam gleam on the shelf!

✳

Cranberry Raspberry Jam

This is my most popular jam. One woman loads up her car with cases of it before she goes south for the winter. We meet in the supermarket parking lot. I fill her trunk. She fills my pockets. Sometimes I wonder what other people must think as they watch this exchange. She tells me that one case goes for presents. Another stays at home. She's my first customer of the season when I reappear at the farmers' market. This year I experimented by putting ⅓ cup of triple sec liqueur in a batch of this jam. Voilà! Another instant success. That's the joy of jam making. New flavors; new combinations; new customers.

1 cup chopped, fresh or frozen unsweetened cranberries
3 cups whole, fresh or frozen unsweetened raspberries
2 tablespoons lemon juice
1½ packages powdered pectin
8 cups sugar

Combine the cranberries, raspberries and lemon juice in a large nonreactive pot. Bring to a boil. Add the pectin. Return to the boil. Add the sugar slowly, stirring constantly. Bring to the boil again and boil for 1 minute, or until the jam sheets off the spoon. When ready, pour into hot, sterilized jars. Cover with new, clean, hot caps. (See section in introduction on jar and cover preparation, pages 24–25.) Invert for 5 minutes.

Makes 7–8 eight-ounce jars

Cranberry Lime Jam

This is not sweet jam. It is beautiful, tangy and just right on banana bread. A small jar tucked into a Christmas basket is a beautiful seasonal surprise.

4 cups chopped, fresh or frozen unsweetened cranberries
1 cup lime pulp (see Lime Marmalade, page 81)
1 package powdered pectin
7 cups sugar

Combine the cranberries and lime pulp in a large nonreactive pot. Bring to a boil. Add the pectin. Return to the boil. Add the sugar slowly, stirring constantly. Bring to the boil again and boil for 1 minute, or until the jam sheets off the spoon. Pour into hot, sterilized jars. Cover with new, clean, hot caps. (See section in introduction on jar and cover preparation, pages 24–25.) Invert for 5 minutes.

Makes 7–8 eight-ounce jars

Cranberry Peach Jam

This might seem like a strange combination. Sweet peaches smooth out the bitterness of the cranberries. The resulting jam is almost coral-colored. I like this as a topping on warm bread pudding. Don't chop the peaches too fine. This needs to have some crunch.

3 cups peeled, pitted and chopped peaches
1 cup chopped, fresh or frozen unsweetened cranberries
2 tablespoons lemon juice
1 ½ packages powdered pectin
8 cups sugar

Combine the peaches, cranberries and lemon juice in a large non-reactive pot. Bring to a boil. Add the pectin. Return to the boil. Add the sugar slowly, stirring constantly. Bring to the boil again and boil for 1 minute, or until the jam sheets off the spoon. Pour into hot, sterilized jars. Cover with new, hot, clean caps. (See section in introduction on jar and cover preparation, pages 24–25.) Invert for 5 minutes.

Makes 8–9 eight-ounce jars

Cranberry Raspberry with Triple Sec Jam

3 cups whole, fresh or frozen unsweetened raspberries
1 cup chopped, fresh or frozen unsweetened cranberries
2 tablespoons lemon juice
1 ½ packages powdered pectin
8 cups sugar
⅓ cup triple sec liqueur

Combine the raspberries, cranberries and lemon juice in a large nonreactive pot. Bring to a boil. Add the pectin. Return to the boil. Add the sugar slowly, stirring constantly. Boil for 1 minute. Add the triple sec. Bring to the boil again and boil for 1 minute, or until the jam sheets off the spoon. Pour into hot, sterilized jars. Cover with new, clean, hot caps. (See section in introduction on jar and cover preparation, pages 24–25.) Invert for 5 minutes.

Makes 7–8 eight-ounce jars

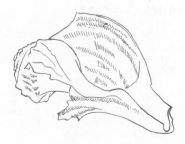

Plum Delicious

IT'S NO USE. I've whistled "The Spring Song." I've imitated the call of the cardinal. I've gotten down on my knees and planted peas on St. Patrick's Day, as prescribed. I've gingerly pulled mulch away from the gardens, looking anxiously for any sign of a crocus or daffodil. I've put orange halves out for the Baltimore orioles. I've cut forsythia branches to force into bloom in the house. In short, I've done everything in my power to nudge spring into existence. It's just no use.

On Cape Cod, spring can be an illusion born of seemingly endless gray days. Chilled by cold air blowing across still-frigid ocean waters, the Cape, like any watery environment, warms up slowly.

Eventually even *our* bones warm up. The sun does come out; the peas pop up and the buds begin to swell. Then true-blue, dyed-in-the-wool Cape Codders start ruminating about the possibility that this might be a good beach plum year. Beach plums are fickle. Just as you think you've found the mother lode of bushes, they disappear. One year they produce prolifically, the next not at all. Everybody has an explanation. "The bees couldn't pollinate . . . too rainy." "The bees couldn't pollinate . . . too cold." "The bees couldn't pollinate . . . the blossoms fell off too soon in that storm." "The bees couldn't pollinate . . . too hot."

When the bees, sun, air, incantations and worship ceremonies please the Goddess of Beach Plums, we have fruit.

Beach plum bushes grow among the sand dunes, along the edges of roads—in any sandy location. They have long, strong taproots that go deep into the water table. They mature slowly, which only adds to their mystique. Eventually they grow big and gnarled. They love to grow among the poison ivy, or perhaps it's the other way around. In any case, where there are beach plums, there is poison ivy. This just makes the challenge greater. The big beach plum bush at the end of my driveway is ancient, its branches touching the ground, bent and twisted. I check it frequently, silently imploring it to produce for me. Last year it did, not a lot, but enough to make several jars. I kept them for myself.

Beach plums bloom before they leaf out. The branches are profusely covered with tiny white blossoms. Clouds come to rest. I dust off my binoculars, get a pad of paper, local road maps, a pen and start the fun. Like an old-fashioned scavenger hunt, the object is to find bushes in bloom, locate and write down the location of the bush and keep your fingers crossed.

There are always disappointments. The best stand of bushes last year is now a house; the ones along the back road that once were so fruitful are now afflicted by a blight; the ones planted at my old house are now beyond my gleaning. And don't ask anyone where they find their beach plums. They won't tell you. Oh, they'll smile that Cheshire cat grin, lower their eyes and mutter something about some field down some nonexistent road. Don't believe them. It's a ruse to make you stop asking. Even I don't divulge my sources. All summer long I check the bushes, watching for the tiny green plums that tell me it's going to be a good year. In early fall, it's time to harvest the plums.

There is a stretch of road near what we used to call the

dump, now called the transfer station, that is lined with bushes. When the time is ripe, I go. I choose the plums that still have a reddish glow, for if I pick them too ripe they may rot before I can use them. Ones with a reddish blush release the most pectin and make the best-tasting jam.

Last year we had no beach plums. None at all. Not one. The year before you couldn't give them away. I ended up with two hundred pounds of them in my freezer. I felt pretty smug. They were all gone by this year. But still the tourists ask for beach plum jam. And when you tell them that there were no beach plums last year, they look puzzled. It's hard for them to understand that we are not a supermarket.

Beach plums have been harvested and eaten since the first settlers arrived. They've developed an aura. I don't know who started the first rumor that beach plums were special, but the propaganda has been very successful. We all scramble to get as many as we can.

Now as I sit selling jam at the local farmers' market, I swap stories with my customers about where the best plums are and if we are going to have any this year. And they smile that covert smile of a true berry scrounger and mutter something about a patch of bushes down an old road. . . .

Some people prefer to cook up beach plums and then hang them in a jelly bag over a bowl to let the juices drip out. You can't squeeze the bag because that would cloud the juice and the clearer the jelly the better. This juice is used to make jelly. It has no pulp. I make jam. I cover several cups of plums with water and cook them slowly until mushy. Then I put them through a Foley Food Mill, pressing out the pulp and juice, leaving behind the pits and skins. It's harder than just letting the juices drip out, but the resulting jam is thick and tangy.

Beach plums are also used to make a soul-warming brandy or, if truth be told, a soul-warming vodka, as well as chutney and other treats to accompany meats, poultry and fish.

When winter winds howl, I pour myself a tiny glass of beach plum cordial and smile that little smile of hidden bushes down a nonexistent road. . . .

Beach Plum Jam

2 tablespoons lemon juice
4 cups beach plum pulp and juice
1 ½ packages powdered pectin
7 cups sugar

Put the lemon juice and beach plum pulp into a deep nonreactive pot. Bring to a boil. Add the pectin. Return to the boil. Add the sugar slowly, stirring constantly. Bring to the boil again and boil for 1 minute, or until the jam sheets off the spoon. Skim off any foam. Pour into hot, sterilized jars. Cover with new, clean, hot caps. (See section in introduction on jar and cover preparation, pages 24–25.) Invert for 5 minutes.

Makes 7–8 eight-ounce jars

Beach Plum Cordial

4 cups beach plums
3 cups sugar
A fifth of vodka or brandy (I like it with vodka)

Put the ingredients into a gallon jar. Punch holes in the cover to allow gases to escape. Cover and put the jar in a dark place. Every day shake the jar. After 2 months decant the resulting cordial into a clean jar. Discard the plums. (The birds love them. They get positively tipsy!)

Makes approximately 2 quarts

Wait until it's cold and snowy. Light the woodstove or snuggle up to the fireplace. Pour yourself a glass of deep red, body-warming cordial and remember hot summer days, waves splashing on the shore, yellow-legged birds running along the surf line, children running from bush to bush. It's then I know I'm living exactly where and how I need to live.

The Mystery of Ordinary Moments

I DIDN'T MAKE UP the phrase "the mystery of ordinary moments." I heard it as part of a sermon. It rolled over and around my tongue, scooted around my mental meanderings, flitted in and out of the context of my daily life. It followed me down the bike trail, into the woods, through the marsh and onto the beach. What is mysterious about ordinary moments?

I picked a day—just an ordinary day, filled to the brim.

I lifted the lid of the composter to throw in the garbage. A fat, contented mouse sat on the garbage, eating. It scurried down a hole it had created into the center of its universe. My leftovers were keeping another creature alive. A fleeting, ordinary moment.

A great blue heron was fishing at the edge of the pond. I walked softly, watching that majestic, long-legged bird prance from spot to spot. When it finally spotted me, it flew off, crying a goose bump–raising call; a prehistoric pterodactyl. A fleeting, ordinary moment.

Walking alone along the edge of the ocean on a blustery afternoon, nobody in sight for miles, I spotted a seal. Popping its silk-smooth gray head up, it looked as curiously at me as I at it. No need for a wet suit, as it dove, disappeared and then reappeared several yards downshore. An extraordinary moment.

I found a wild apple on the ground. Not perfect, not round. Some worm holes, some brown spots. I ate it. An ordinary moment.

It was then that I remembered picking apples at the apple farm when the children were young, teaching them that apples didn't come from plastic bags in the market. Watching them run from tree to tree, being helped to climb a few steps up the stepladder to pluck a rosy one from a dwarf tree, planted just so little hands could reach high enough.

Coming home with half a bushel of fruit, wondering how on earth we'd ever eat all those apples. Pushing chairs close to the table so each little one could have a turn pushing the cooked apples through the food mill, making applesauce. Watching the wonder on expectant faces as they ate the first food they'd ever "cooked."

Now, my grandson Jason, age four, when asked, tells me, "I picked a *gorgeous* McIntosh and a *beautiful* yellow Delicious apple." He describes in detail how he uses a picker, a contraption made with a long handle with a basket arrangement at the top.

"You *capture* the apple in the basket, twist the basket and the apple falls into the basket, Grandma."

Those new, grand words. A wonderful, ordinary moment!

I've solved the mystery. I breathe. I see. I hear.

I've picked apples on a warm fall day surrounded by the trilling voices of children.

＊

Apple Raspberry Jam

1 cup whole, fresh or frozen unsweetened raspberries
3 cups unsweetened applesauce
3 tablespoons lemon juice
1 ½ packages powdered pectin
7 cups sugar

Combine the raspberries, applesauce and lemon juice in a large nonreactive pot. Bring to a boil. Add the pectin. Return to the boil. Add the sugar slowly, stirring constantly. Bring to the boil again and boil for 1 minute, or until the jam sheets off the spoon. Pour into hot, sterilized jars. Cover with new, clean, hot caps. (See section in introduction on jar and cover preparation, pages 24–25.) Invert for 5 minutes.

Makes 7–8 eight-ounce jars

Cranberry Apple Jam

3 cups unsweetened applesauce
1 cup chopped, fresh or frozen unsweetened cranberries
3 tablespoons lemon juice
1 ½ packages powdered pectin
7 cups sugar
¼–½ cup water, depending on how thick the applesauce is

Combine the applesauce, cranberries and lemon juice in a large nonreactive pot. Bring to a boil. Add the pectin. Return to the boil. Add the sugar slowly, stirring constantly. If the jam seems to be very thick, add a little of the water. Be careful not to water down the jam too much. It won't jell. Bring to the boil once again and boil for 1 minute, or until the jam sheets off the spoon. Pour into hot, sterilized jars. Cover with new, clean, hot caps. (See section in introduction on jar and cover preparation, pages 24–25.) Invert for 5 minutes.

Makes 7–8 eight-ounce jars

Meditation on a Crab Apple Theme

MY FRIENDS RANDY AND PAUL have a bed-and-breakfast in Brewster, and send me their overflow. Their overflow keeps my bed-and-breakfast operation solvent. Their generosity even extends to the crab apple tree in their yard. I don't tell them that picking my own fruit plants my feet solidly on the earth, forces me to slow down, breathe deeply, pick gently . . . reconnects me to my beginnings. Such friends!

Ripe crab apples hanging from green-leafed stems; Christmas ornaments in September. I stretch as high as I can, gently pulling the branches closer. The air is soft, the sky bright, bright blue, the maples and oaks not quite ready to turn. The pond nearby mirrors the sky. Duck families, now grown, scoot back and forth.

This gentle day is a gift. Each day is a gift. Sometimes the quiescent volcano that is my grief rumbles; threatens to erupt. It's then that I try to just observe this sadness and let it go. It's not easy when the sun is bright, the air soft and memories powerful.

The first fruit falls noisily into the bucket. By the time I've filled the bucket, the apples fall soundlessly. My meditation is complete.

A bite of this very small apple dispels any illusions that "pretty" is by definition sweet. They are not. They are mouth-puckering sour, thus the "crab." The jam, however, is gorgeous in flavor and in color.

Crab Apple Jam

Harvest your apples. Cut them up and put them in a deep pot. Cover with water, so you can still see the apples through the water, about 1 inch above the top of the apples. When the apples are soft, put through a Foley Food Mill. Then take:

4 cups apple pulp
2 tablespoons lemon juice
1 ½ packages powdered pectin
8 cups sugar

Put the apple pulp and lemon juice in a large nonreactive pot. Bring to a boil. Add the pectin. Return to the boil. Add the sugar slowly, stirring constantly. Bring to the boil again and boil for 1 minute, or until the jam sheets off the spoon. Pour into hot, sterilized jars. Cover with new, clean, hot caps. (See section in introduction on jar and cover preparation, pages 24–25.) Invert for 5 minutes.

Makes 8–9 eight-ounce jars

The jam is almost scarlet. The taste is tangy. Just right for zucchini bread.

Winter

When the Wild
Geese Fly

When the deer is bedded down,
And the bear has gone to ground
And the Northern goose has wandered off
To warmer bay and sound,
It's so easy in the cold to feel
The darkness of the year,
And the heart is growing lonely for
The Morning.
When the darkness falls around you
And the North wind comes to blow,
And you hear him call your name out
As he walks the brittle snow,
That old wind don't mean you trouble,
He don't care or even know,
He's just walking down the darkness
Towards the Morning.
It's a pity we don't know
What the little flowers know
They can't face the cold November
They can't take the ice and snow.

They put their glories all behind them
Bow their heads and let it go;
But you know they'll be there shining in
The Morning.
Oh my Joanie, don't you know
That the stars are swinging slow
And the seas are rolling easy,
As they did so long ago.
And if I had a thing to give you
I would tell you one more time
That the world is always turning towards the morning.

—Gordon Bok, "Turning Toward the
Morning"

On Cape Cod, spectacular, heart-gripping fall eases into winter. It's usually not dramatic. The days become shorter. The tourists are gone. There are fewer cars on the road. The pine needles have fallen, turning roads and paths a crunchy golden brown. My load of firewood gets delivered and stacked; the porch furniture gets put away and I reluctantly take apart my bed on the porch and go back inside to sleep. Just as reluctantly, I turn off the water to the outside shower. It's time to move indoors.

Ocean waters that have taken so long to warm up cool down slowly. In fact, the warmest waters of the season are in September. It's just the air that's so nippy!

I listen for the Canadian geese. Honking their arrival, they descend on the pond. Sometimes fifty or more are there, quietly swimming around, communicating with each other. When they take off, I can hear the whoosh of their wings as they fly low overhead, honking loudly. The sound never fails to evoke in me the sense that perhaps I too should be migrating, should be joining the "snow birds"—those people who, as soon as the days grow short, leave, like the birds, for warmer climes.

I stay.

Now it's time to put round brown bulbs into the ground. Squatting, bending and digging, I repeat my annual ritual, a ritual that tells me that I will be here in the morning when those brown bulbs burst forth into waves of daffodils and marching armies of tulips. It is a miracle that never fails to astonish me. How such a simple, repetitive act can, in a few months, reap such glorious, soul-affirming rewards.

I turn to the beaches as the days grow colder. Beaches that parking restrictions made off-limits during the summer are accessible. Like greeting an old friend, I clamber down the dunes. The beaches stretch for endless miles. Summer soft sand has been sculpted by northeast wind–driven waves, leaving frozen designs in the sand, making walking easy. Wintering-over sandpipers dash back and forth following the waves as they crash up on the beach, leaving behind tiny delectable edibles. The dog literally grins as she's allowed to run along the beach, pretending she's a fierce warrior as she chases the birds.

At Duck Harbor in Wellfleet, on the bay side, where in summer the sun shines with a Mediterranean intensity, brine ice forms into wondrous icebergs that wash up on the beach and pile up in the bay like huge building blocks gone haywire. Deceptive-looking, they are squishy when you walk on them. Sometimes the cold is so intense, as only wet cold can be, that film breaks in the camera. On those days I bundle up so only my eyes are uncovered.

Now is also the best time to gather rocks. The last vestiges of the glaciers that ended up in the moraine that is the Cape are stones of every description, sculpted by waves and sand. A friend brought me stones from Alaska to compare with the ones on the Cape. They are identical! Imagine the natural events that brought those stones here. Sometimes I pick only white ones. Those are the ones on my windowsill over the sink. Almost always elliptical and very smooth, they make good "worry stones." I can touch them anytime I need to. Sometimes I need larger stones—those which are conglomerates of different kinds of rock, fused by some cataclysmic event eons and eons ago. These stones I've carried from one place to another, packing them in boxes each time I've moved. Some I've had for more than thirty years. They rest on a table, available to be turned over and over, as I turn memories over and over.

Along with the winter come the seed catalogs. No fools those seed people! They know just when it feels as if winter will last for years; just when you've shoveled as many times as your body will allow and still it snows; just when it's rained for many days and then frozen; just as you want to eat some spicy exotic food and every eatery has "closed for the season."

I pile the catalogs up and proceed to indulge in my favorite fantasy. What can I grow this year that I've never attempted before? I write and rewrite the order slips. I calculate what it's going to cost and then rationalize by saying that each $50 I spend on seeds is $50 less that I'll have to spend on a therapist! The seed orders go out, and one day when the ground is clear and free of snow, I lug in two sawhorses and a four-by-eight-foot plywood plank. I set up my seed-starting table in front of my south-facing windows. I always start too soon. My tomatoes are ready to go outside weeks before it's warm enough. My marigolds have buds when the ground is still cold. No matter. I have a wonderful time making sure I'll be ready when it finally warms up.

This is the time of year when I put aside the recipes of summer, and along with the pot of simmering stew or mushroom barley soup, I start my winter recipes. It's easy to find the time. It's pitch dark by 5 P.M.

✳

Exotica Blueberry Pondica

WHEN THE WINTER winds howl and the snow flies, Blueberry Pond looks dark and restless. The tupelo trees have long since shed their scarlet leaves. Only the wintering-over geese are left, gray, brown and black, head under wing, one leg under chest feathers, huddled on the shore. If the pond freezes, they too will head for open water.

When the pond freezes, it takes on a wonderful new dimension. It gleams and glistens. What looked ominous is now playful. Neighborhood children come down to skate or slide. Visiting grandchildren walk out to the center—far enough to be brave, close enough to call out, "Look at *me*."

It's chutney time. Thick and spicy, chutney conjures up exotic, faraway places. Indian princes and Moroccan sheiks rise in fragrant clouds from the bubbling pot. Exotica on Blueberry Pondica!

In the freezer are bags labeled chutney. They contain cut-up mangos, peaches, melons and other fruits. What makes chutney wonderful is the combining of unusual flavors—spices and vinegar, brown sugar and raisins, sweet red peppers and hot preserved ginger. The smell of cooking chutney fills the house. You can practically see the genie in the rising steam! I put aside ample jars for my friend and chutney aficionado Jim Robinson. He's been in India and tasted the "real" thing. He says mine is the best he's ever eaten!

Apple Chutney

10 *cups cut-up, firm pie or cooking apples*
4 *cups cider vinegar*
6 *cups brown sugar*
1 *cup raisins*
1 *sweet red pepper, chopped*
1 *cup chopped preserved ginger (more to taste)*
1 *tablespoon Chinese chili bean paste**
The following dried spices tied up in cheesecloth:
   3 cinnamon sticks
   8–10 whole cloves
   8–10 whole allspice
   6 cardamom pods

Combine the ingredients in a deep pot. Bring to a boil. Reduce the heat and simmer, stirring to make sure the chutney does not stick to the bottom of the pot. Continue to cook until the chutney is thick. This can take up to 2 hours. After about an hour you can remove the spice packet. When the chutney is thick, pour it into hot, sterilized jars. Cover with new, clean, hot caps. (See section in introduction on jar and cover preparation, pages 24–25.) Process in a boiling water bath for 10 minutes. (See section in introduction on processing chutney, pages 27–28.)

    Remove from water. Tighten caps. Cool on a rack. Store in a cool, dark place.

Makes 10–12 *eight-ounce jars*

Chinese chili bean paste can be obtained from specialty food stores or any oriental market.

Mixed Fruit Chutney

My friend Tom is the executive chef at a local restaurant. It's a new job for him. His other, much more satisfying job is operating a greenhouse with his wife, Kris. It's no ordinary greenhouse. Everything in it is grown hydroponically. No dirt. All kinds of lettuce and oriental greens sprout up out of holes in row upon row of tubes through which run nutrients and water. The sound of running water greets your ears when you enter. It's a tropical delight in the middle of winter.

One day Tom asked me if I made chutney. He then wanted to taste some to see if it was good enough to feed to his patrons. "Tastes professional" was his verdict.

"I beg your pardon. I'm a professional; my chutney is professional. How much do you need?" I gulped when he said, "A gallon a week."

I went to the local cook shop, bought a very big pot, some very large containers, and started cooking. Tom tells me that patrons now ask what kind of chutney is being served when they order. Some he serves with venison, some with turkey, some with duck or pork. Both of us are scrambling to think up new ways to serve my magic potions as the genie tries mightily to escape the pot! This recipe is a combination of fruits, all of which have interesting flavors.

To make the mixed fruit chutney:

1 large box pitted prunes
1 pound dried apricots
2 cups chopped apples
2 cups whole, fresh or frozen unsweetened cranberries
2 chopped oranges, with skin
6 cups brown sugar
4 cups cider vinegar
1 cup chopped preserved ginger
The following dried spices tied up in cheesecloth:
  3 cinnamon sticks
  8–10 whole cloves
  8–10 whole allspice
  6 cardamom pods
*1 tablespoon Chinese chili bean paste**

Soak the prunes and apricots in a bowl with enough water to cover them. When they have swelled and are soft, chop them in your food processor. Be careful not to make mush. You want to have some chunks.

Combine the prunes and apricots with all the other ingredients except the chili bean paste in a large pot and cook until thick, and the spices have had a chance to permeate the chutney, about 2 hours. Slow cooking also allows the taste of the vinegar to dissipate. Remove the spice packet after about an hour. During the last few minutes of cooking add the chili bean paste.

Chinese chili bean paste can be obtained from specialty food stores or any oriental market.

This is not a particularly sweet chutney. The oranges and cranberries give it a wonderful tangy flavor. When fully cooked, pour into hot, sterilized jars. Cover with new, clean, hot caps. (See section in introduction on jar and cover preparation, pages 24–25.) Process for 10 minutes in a boiling water bath. (See section in introduction on processing chutney, pages 27–28.)

Remove from water. Tighten covers. Cool on a rack. Store in a cool place.

Makes 10–12 eight-ounce jars

Mango Chutney

I don't grow mangos. I'm not even remotely near anyplace where they grow. When Len and I spent some time in the Florida Everglades, we found a small stand that sold mango drinks, mango jam and fresh, locally grown mangos. It *almost* made me want to move to south Florida.

When I went to Costa Rica in 1992 with a group of women, trying to learn how to travel alone, I ate mangos three times a day. Mangos and I have an intimate relationship. Relishing the sweet flesh left clinging to the seed after I've cut away the main part of the fruit, I ignore the juice trickling down my chin. Loading up on vitamin C. It's a good excuse to be a glutton.

12 large mangos, peeled
4 cups cider vinegar
6 cups brown sugar
1 sweet red pepper, chopped
1 cup raisins
1 cup chopped preserved ginger
1 tablespoon Chinese chili bean paste*
The following dried spices tied up in cheesecloth:

    3 cinnamon sticks

    8–10 whole cloves

    8–10 whole allspice

    6 cardamom pods

*Chinese chili bean paste can be obtained from specialty food stores or any oriental market.

Slice the flesh from the peeled mangos. Discard the large pit. Chop the mango flesh in your food processor. Remember to leave it chunky.

Combine with the other ingredients. Cook in a large pot until thick, for about 2 hours, stirring occasionally to prevent the chutney from sticking to the bottom of the pot. Remove the spice packet after about an hour. When thick enough, pour into hot, sterilized jars. Cover with hot, clean caps that have not been used before. (See section in introduction on jar and cover preparation, pages 24–25.) Process in a boiling water bath for 10 minutes. (See section in introduction on processing chutney, pages 27–28.) Remove from water. Tighten caps. Allow to cool. Store in a cool, dark place.

Makes 10–12 eight-ounce jars

Chutney is about interesting combinations, so experiment. I've used cranberries, peaches, mangos, rhubarb, prunes, oranges and melons—all kinds of exotic treats.

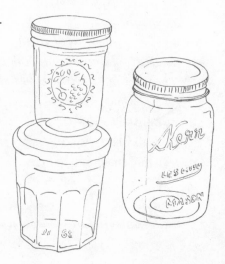

Green Tomato Chutney

In late fall, when the threat of a frost is imminent, comes the gardener's ultimate test—what to do with the baskets and baskets of green tomatoes that will never ripen on the vine. Some can be wrapped individually in either tissue or newspaper, and put in a single layer in a box in a cool, dark place, where they will ripen slowly.

Really hard green tomatoes are amazing in chutney. Just make sure the tomatoes have not started to ripen.

10 *cups green tomatoes, cut into chunks*
2 *cups unpeeled and cut-up green apples*
4 *cups brown sugar*
2 *cups cider vinegar*
1 ½ *cups minced onions*
½ *cup chopped preserved ginger*
2 *teaspoons ground cinnamon*
2 *teaspoons ground coriander*
2 *teaspoons ground allspice*
2 *tablespoons mustard seed*
1 *tablespoon Chinese chili bean paste (optional)**

Mix all the ingredients except the chili bean paste in a deep non-reactive pot. Bring to a boil, stirring constantly, to prevent the chutney from scorching. Lower the heat to a simmer, and continue to cook and stir until the chutney is thick, 45 minutes to 1 hour. If you want it a bit spicier, you can add the chili bean paste.

*Chinese chili bean paste can be obtained from specialty food stores or any oriental market.

When the chutney is thick, pour into hot, sterilized jars and cover with new, clean, hot caps. (See section in introduction on jar and cover preparation, pages 24–25.) Process for 10 minutes in a boiling water bath. (See section in introduction on processing chutney, pages 27–28.) Remove from water and tighten covers. Allow to cool. Store in a cool place.

Makes 10–12 eight-ounce jars

Plum Chutney

When my children were young, they used to call Italian prune plums "sad plums," the result of hearing me call them tragedy plums. Whatever you call them, the little dark purple plums that reach the market in the fall make wonderful chutney. This chutney is particularly good with a pork roast.

10 cups chopped purple plums
4 cups cider vinegar
6 cups brown sugar
1 cup chopped preserved ginger
The following dried spices tied up in cheesecloth:
    3 cinnamon sticks
    8–10 whole cloves
    8–10 whole allspice
    6 cardamom pods
1 tablespoon Chinese chili bean paste*

Put the ingredients in a large nonreactive pot. Simmer until thick, approximately 1–2 hours, depending on how ripe the plums are. When thick, pour into hot, sterilized jars. (See section in introduction on jar and cover preparation, pages 24–25.) Make sure the covers are on securely but not too tight. Process in a boiling water bath for 10 minutes. (See section in introduction on processing chutney, pages 27–28.) Remove from water. Tighten covers. Allow to cool. Store in a cool location.

Makes 10–12 eight-ounce jars

*Chinese chili bean paste can be obtained from specialty food stores or any oriental market.

Cranberry Orange Chutney

4 cups cider vinegar
6 cups brown sugar
The following dried spices tied up in cheesecloth:
  3 cinnamon sticks
  8–10 whole cloves
  8–10 whole allspice
  6 cardamom pods
8 cups whole, fresh or frozen unsweetened cranberries
2 cups orange sections
1 cup raisins
½ cup chopped preserved ginger (more to taste)

Put vinegar, brown sugar and spice packet in a large nonreactive pot. Chop the cranberries and oranges in a food processor until quite mushy. Add to pot. Cook on low heat for 1 hour, stirring to prevent sticking. Add the raisins and ginger. Remove the spice packet. Continue to cook until thick.

Pour into hot, sterilized jars. Cover with new, clean, hot caps. (See section in introduction on jar and cover preparation, pages 24–25.) Process in a boiling water bath for 10 minutes. (See section in introduction on processing chutney, pages 27–28.) Remove from bath. Tighten covers. Allow cooling. Store in a cool place.

Makes 10–12 eight-ounce jars

Cranberry Citrus Chutney

This chutney is an instant success at the annual Sea Captains' Fair at First Parish in Brewster, Massachusetts. The following recipe will give you 6 cups. You can easily double it. My thanks to Ellen Barber.

½ cup cider vinegar
2¼ cups firmly packed light brown sugar
1 teaspoon curry powder
½ teaspoon ground ginger
¼ teaspoon ground cloves
¼ teaspoon ground allspice
½ teaspoon ground cinnamon
1½ cups cranberry juice cocktail
2 limes, rind grated, pith discarded and fruit
    cut into sections
2 navel oranges, rind grated, pith discarded and fruit
    cut into sections
1 tart apple, peeled, cored and coarsely chopped
6 cups whole, fresh or frozen unsweetened cranberries
½ cup raisins
½ cup chopped dried apricots
½ cup chopped walnuts

In a large stainless steel pot, combine vinegar, sugar, spices and cranberry juice. Bring to a boil, stirring until the sugar is dissolved. Add the lime and orange rinds and sections. Add apple. Simmer the mixture, stirring, for 10 minutes.

Add 3 cups of the cranberries, raisins and apricots. Simmer, stirring occasionally, for 30–40 minutes, or until thick.

Stir in 2 cups of the remaining cranberries. Simmer for another 10 minutes. Stir in remaining cup of cranberries and walnuts. Simmer and stir for 15 minutes.

Pour into hot, sterilized jars. Cover with new, clean, hot caps. (See section in introduction on jar and cover preparation, pages 24–25.) Process in a boiling water bath for 10 minutes. (See section in introduction on processing chutney, pages 27–28.) Remove from water. Tighten caps. Allow to cool. Store in a cool place.

Makes 6 eight-ounce jars

Mozart and Marmalade

IN HER BOOK *Stones for Ibarra,** Harriet Doerr writes, "Memories are like corks left out of bottles. They swell. They no longer fit."

How true! I am aware that it is easy to remember selectively, to create out of whole cloth someone who may have never existed. Gone are the frustrations of daily living: the arguments, the hurt feelings, the pettiness, the misconstrued communications. What remain are the images; the edges now round, the hurtfulness now soft memories. So it was for the first two years after Len died. When he died in 1991 the cork that was his life swelled out of the bottle and I, unable to push the cork back in, had to come to grips with what was my new reality and what realistically was my memory of him.

Mozart became my therapist. Night after night, as I struggled to understand my loss, as I swam up from the deepest chasms of despair and longing, I would take out my jam pots, gather my tools and make jam. Night after night Mozart accompanied me on my journey. Not any Mozart. Mozart's Requiem became my talisman. All the longing, all the soaring melodies, all the poignant harmonies, all flooded my soul. When the first CD got scratched and started skipping, I bought a new one, panicky at the thought of not hearing the music clearly.

Then one night I found myself singing along. No longer did I weep every time I put on the music. Finally . . . finally I was able to see the pots clearly, rather than through a veil of tears. And

*Harriet Doerr, Stones for Ibarra (New York: Viking, 1984), p. 3.

what I discovered was that the Requiem took just the right amount of time to make a batch of marmalade! Marmalade—tangy, bittersweet, filled with little tough strands. Marmalade came to represent what my life was in reality—bittersweet with tough strands.

In *The Book of Marmalade,** C. Anne Wilson explores the origins of the word "marmalade." Marmalade first arrived in England from Spain and Portugal when sailors brought over a local conserve made from quinces, called *marmelo,* and sugar. In fact, she reports that the earliest Greek and Roman physicians prescribed concoctions of quinces as an aid to digestion. Even earlier physicians stored quinces tightly packed in honey jars. The ensuing mass was then called *melomeli* by the Greeks, and from this beginning came marmalade.

Over time, I too have experimented with all kinds of combinations. I still call them all marmalade: grapefruit with ginger, cranberry orange marmalade, orange marmalade with brandy, apricot orange, apple orange breakfast spread, five-fruit, four-fruit, pineapple orange, lime. I make a lot of marmalade! Mozart still accompanies me on my journey. I never make marmalade without the Requiem, but recently I've made a few additions. I've added Gregorian chants to my marmalade making, and as I stir, I can visualize rows of hooded monks singing their praises. Mozart would understand.

My life is still tangy. Tangy with vitality. Tangy with zest, and a lusty appreciation of life, the little tough strands now easier to swallow.

*C. Anne Wilson, The Book of Marmalade (New York: St. Martin's, 1985).

Lime Marmalade*

Remember those romance novels set in the South in the early twentieth century? Voluptuous young women, handsome and dashing young men, all dressed in white, walking down some garden path, gin and tonic in hand? Although limes make me think of summer, white dresses and southern plantations, I make lime marmalade in the winter, when limes are readily available. When I eat lime marmalade, I too can be a southern belle from a bygone era.

Limes, incongruously colored fruit, provide a zesty addition to jams and marmalades, as well as many other fruit combinations.

10 limes
Water

Day 1: Wash the limes. With your zester, remove the peel, being careful not to get any of the white pith (the layer under the peel) when you are taking off the peel. Remove the white pith and discard.

Cut the limes into very thin slices, and then cut the slices into smaller pieces. Do not chop up.

Pour the limes and juice into a measuring cup. Add an equal amount of water.

Bring to a boil in a large nonreactive pot and simmer for 10 minutes. Turn off the heat. Allow to sit overnight.

From Madelaine Bullwinkel, Gourmet Preserves Chez Madelaine *(Chicago: Contemporary Books, 1984), p. 117.*

Day 2: Repeat this cooking process.

At this point, you can do several things. I sometimes put the lime pulp into a container and refrigerate. Then, when I want to make a jam that has lime in it, I simply take some of the lime "mush," add it to my recipe and continue on.

Day 3: If you want to make lime marmalade, reheat the limes once more. You should have about a quart of lime pulp. If not, add enough water to make 4 cups.

4 cups lime pulp
7 cups sugar

Simmer for 10 minutes, being very careful not to overcook. This marmalade stiffens up very easily. The marmalade is ready to process when it sheets off the spoon or develops a skin when put on a cold plate in the refrigerator for 10 minutes. Pour into clean, hot sterilized jars. Cover with new, clean, hot caps. (See section in introduction on jar and cover preparation, pages 24–25.) Invert for 5 minutes. The marmalade may take a day or two to firm up. Don't panic.

M*akes 8–9 eight-ounce jars*

It's delicious on cranberry nut bread or date nut bread. I keep a jar of half-processed lime pulp in the refrigerator all the time. I never know when I'm going to get the urge to put raspberries and limes or apricots and limes together. Lime marmalade conjures up the Florida Everglades, roseate spoonbills and pelicans diving into Florida Bay. Not a bad way to repress snow, cold and ice.

Apple Orange Breakfast Spread

Some friends came home from Maine with a jar of jam for me. That tends to happen. Kind of like bringing coals to Newcastle. "Eat it, and see if you can reproduce it. We think it'll sell well."

I ate the whole jar, slowly, rolling the flavors around on my tongue. A little spicy, a little tangy, a little sweet. It's not a bad way to test out something new. Just eat it straight.

I decided I'd call this jam Apple Orange Breakfast Spread. You can call it anything you want. It's very good on French toast or pancakes. It's not a particularly good selling jam, though. People buying jam from a vendor at a farmers' market are not necessarily adventurous when it comes to trying new flavors. Those who are brave come back for more, and more.

3 cups cooking apples, peeled (or unsweetened applesauce)
2 large oranges, unpeeled and cut up, with seeds removed
1 cup raisins
1 can frozen apple juice, undiluted
3 cups water
7 cups sugar
1 teaspoon ground cinnamon
1 teaspoon ground mace
1 teaspoon ground nutmeg
1 package powdered pectin

Grind the apples, oranges, raisins and apple juice in a food processor until they are mushy and you can't really distinguish any individual fruit.

Add the remaining ingredients, then bring to a boil in a

large nonreactive pot. Cook until the marmalade sheets off the spoon or develops a skin when put on a cold plate in the refrigerator for 10 minutes. Fill hot, sterilized jars. Cover with new, clean, hot caps. (See section in introduction on jar and cover preparation, pages 24–25.) Invert for 5 minutes.

Makes 10–12 eight-ounce jars

Cranberry Orange Marmalade

This is one of the most requested marmalades. Put a teaspoonful in a cup of orange spice tea. Lather it on warm, homemade oatmeal bread. Not only does this marmalade taste wonderful, it's beautiful!

4 large oranges, unpeeled and cut up, with seeds removed
2 cups fresh or frozen unsweetened cranberries
1 package powdered pectin
1 cup water
12 cups sugar

Chop the oranges and cranberries in your food processor until they are a fine, mushy consistency. Put into a large nonreactive pot and add the remaining ingredients.

Bring to a boil. Reduce heat and simmer for 15–20 minutes, stirring frequently. Place a spoonful of marmalade on a cold plate in the refrigerator for 10 minutes. If the marmalade develops a skin, it's ready. If not, cook for another few minutes and try again.

When ready, pour into hot, sterilized jars. Cover with new, clean, hot caps. (See section in introduction on jar and cover preparation, pages 24–25.) Invert for 5 minutes.

Makes 10–12 eight-ounce jars

There is an alternative way of making this marmalade. You can use Chivers's Ma Made Orange Marmalade Mix (see Appendix). This is a mix made from Seville oranges, which are bitter oranges. To make marmalade using this mix:

1 can Ma Made Orange Marmalade Mix
1 ½ cups water
2 cups finely chopped unsweetened cranberries
1 package powdered pectin
10 cups sugar

Put the ingredients in a large nonreactive pot and bring to a boil. Reduce the heat and simmer, stirring frequently, for 10–15 minutes. Use the cold plate method to determine if the marmalade is ready. When ready, pour into hot, sterilized jars. Cover with new, clean, hot caps. (See section in introduction on jar and cover preparation, pages 24–25.) Invert for 5 minutes.

Makes *10–12 eight-ounce jars*

Lemon Lime Marmalade

Some of my British friends like very bitter marmalade. I've had them try every variety I make. "Too sweet" is the usual comment. Finally, I had them try Lemon Lime. "Just right!" I felt like Goldilocks and the three bears.

Maybe it's the English weather that makes people long for sour marmalade. In any event, this marmalade *is* just right. The limes take some of the edge off the lemons. The lemons make your mouth curl just the right amount. Delicious on English muffins. (What else?)

You can use the three-day method, preparing lemons as you did limes in the recipe for Lime Marmalade (page 81). You will also need to have a supply of lime pulp in the refrigerator.

6 lemons
2 cups lime pulp
10 cups sugar
1 package powdered pectin

Day 1: Wash the lemons. With your zester, remove the peel. Remove the white pith and discard. Cut into thin slices and put in a large nonreactive pot. Add an equal amount of water.

Bring to a boil. Reduce heat and simmer for 5 minutes. Allow to sit overnight.

Day 2: Repeat this cooking process.

Day 3: Add the lime pulp to your lemon pulp. You should have a total of 6 cups of the lemon-lime combination.

Add the sugar, stirring constantly, and pectin. Bring to a boil. Reduce heat and simmer slowly for 10–15 minutes. The marmalade is ready if it develops a skin when put on a cold plate in the refrigerator for 10 minutes. When ready, pour into hot, sterilized jars. Cover with new, clean, hot caps. (See section in introduction on jar and cover preparation, pages 24–25.) Invert for 5 minutes.

Makes 10–12 eight-ounce jars

OR:

1 can Ma Made Lemon Marmalade Mix (see Appendix)
2 cups lime pulp
1 package powdered pectin
1 ½ cups water
12 cups sugar

Put the ingredients in a large nonreactive pot. Bring to a boil. Lower the heat and simmer for 10–15 minutes, or until the marmalade develops a skin when put on a cold plate in the refrigerator for 10 minutes. When ready, pour into hot, sterilized jars. Cover with new, clean, hot caps. (See section in introduction on jar and cover preparation, pages 24–25.) Invert for 5 minutes.

Makes 10–12 eight-ounce jars

Lime Ginger Marmalade

Now that you've become an expert taking the zest off lemons and limes, you can branch out. This recipe combines two of my favorite ingredients, limes and ginger. *Very* British and very refreshing.

4 cups lime pulp (see Lime Marmalade recipe, page 81)
½ cup very finely chopped preserved ginger (more to taste)
1 package powdered pectin
8 cups sugar

Combine the limes, ginger and pectin in a large nonreactive pot. Bring to a boil. Slowly add the sugar, stirring constantly. Return to the boil and boil for 1 minute, or until the marmalade sheets off the spoon or develops a skin when placed on a cold plate in the refrigerator for 10 minutes.

When ready, pour into hot, sterilized jars. Cover with new, clean, hot caps. (See section in introduction on jar and cover preparation, pages 24–25.) Invert for 5 minutes.

Makes 8–9 eight-ounce jars

Grapefruit Ginger Marmalade

Pink grapefruit has a wonderful sweetness that's unexpected, as is that wonderful pink color. You can eat it without sugar. Ginger also has an unexpected sweetness, once you get past the intensity of the flavor. If I lived in Florida, I think I'd haunt the citrus groves, asking for fruit that has dropped to the ground. Then I'd chop up all those grapefruit and stack bags of pulp in my freezer. Instead, I haunt the markets, watching for that time in winter when citrus fruits appear in the fruit section. Eating pink grapefruit is much more satisfying than a vitamin C pill.

This is a three-day marmalade, much like the Lime Marmalade recipe (page 81). Cooking the grapefruit over a three-day period allows the pectin to be released. I add the ginger on the third day.

3 large grapefruit, unpeeled and cut up, with seeds removed
Water
1 package powdered pectin
½–1 cup finely chopped preserved ginger
10–12 cups sugar

Day 1: Chop the grapefruit in your food processor until it becomes a fine pulp. You may need to add a little water to make the processor work more efficiently.

Measure the grapefruit and add an equal amount of water. Bring to a boil in a large nonreactive pot. Reduce the heat and simmer for 15 minutes. Let stand overnight.

Day 2: Repeat this cooking process. Let stand overnight. You should have around 6 cups.

Day 3: Add the pectin and ginger and bring to the boil again. Add the sugar slowly, stirring constantly. Reduce heat and simmer for approximately 10 minutes. The marmalade is ready if it develops a skin when put on a cold plate in the refrigerator for 10 minutes. When ready, pour into hot, sterilized jars. Cover with new, clean, hot caps. (See section in introduction on jar and cover preparation, pages 24–25.) Invert for 5 minutes.

Makes 10–12 eight-ounce jars

Five-Fruit Marmalade

1 pineapple, cored and cut into chunks
2 limes, unpeeled and cut into chunks
2 lemons, unpeeled and cut into chunks
1 grapefruit, unpeeled and cut into chunks
2 oranges, unpeeled and cut into chunks
3–4 cups water, depending on how thick you want
  the marmalade
8–10 cups sugar*
1 package powdered pectin

Remove all the seeds from the citrus fruits.

Chop up the fruits in a food processor. Do not overload it. The fruit should have a finely chopped, almost mushy consistency.

Put all the fruit in a large nonreactive pot. Add the remaining ingredients and bring to a boil. Reduce heat and simmer for 10 minutes. Turn off the heat. Let stand overnight. The next day, simmer again for 10–15 minutes, or until a spoonful of marmalade develops a skin when placed on a cold plate in the refrigerator for 10 minutes. When the marmalade is ready, pour into hot, sterilized jars. Cover with new, clean, hot caps. (See section in introduction on jar and cover preparation, pages 24–25). Invert for 5 minutes. Leave on a rack to cool. Store in a cool place.

Makes 11–12 eight-ounce jars

*8 cups for each 4 cups of prepared fruit. Use more sugar if you have more fruit.

Five-fruit marmalade is vintage marmalade—tangy, sweet and bitter all rolled into one. It's particularly good on Irish soda bread, English muffins and, believe it or not, peanut butter sandwiches.

You can make four-fruit marmalade by leaving out the pineapple and adjusting the water and sugar amounts according to how much chopped fruit you have.

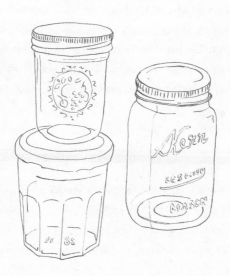

Orange Marmalade
with Whiskey

This marmalade is a favorite with an Englishwoman who comes to visit her children each summer. She takes marmalade back to England. I'm honored. I thought marmalade was invented in England. I don't tell her that I use Irish whiskey.

1 can Ma Made Orange Marmalade Mix*
1 ½ cups water
9 cups sugar
⅓ cup Irish whiskey

Follow the directions on the Ma Made can. Just before pouring, add the whiskey. Bring back to the boil.

Pour into hot, sterilized jars. (See section in introduction on jar and cover preparation, pages 24-25.) Cover with new, clean, hot caps. Invert for 5 minutes. Store in a cool place.

Makes 8–9 eight-ounce jars

*See section on Ma Made Orange Marmalade Mix in the Appendix. It can be purchased in food catalogs such as Williams-Sonoma or Vermont Country Store.

Spring

Spring Song

THE TRAYS OF TINY PLANTS reach for the sun streaming in the south-facing windows of my dining room. I had read all the seed catalogs from cover to cover, and in the deep winter of February started my seeds. Starting seeds each year is an affirmation that spring will come. Starting seeds each year is reproduction and renewal. Starting seeds each year is my silent pledge that I will be here in April; that I am competent . . . I can survive. That I can pay attention to more moments and not worry about the whole month or year . . . or the rest of my life. It's a lesson hard taught and harder to maintain in the dead of winter. April has come—according to the calendar, that is. On the rare, really sunny day, the plants in the window need extra watering. I turn them around so the drooping stems straighten out as the plants turn toward the sun.

On a nice warm day, I do the same thing. I go to a protected spot, prop my back against a seawall and rotate. That first caress of warmth striking my face slides down into the deepest recesses of my soul. I've made it through another winter.

Generally, the ocean, which was so slow to cool down, is just as reluctant to heat up. The prevailing easterly winds bring gray days and cold rains. We warm up, leaf out and get spring weeks after the trees are in full flower inland.

Restless, in need of a "spring tonic," I have a tendency to pull aside the mulch that has covered the bulbs all winter. I need to see green! Finally, the day comes when the first green sprouts of the daffodils, tulips and grape hyacinths peek out. Then I worry about the early spring snowstorm that inevitably tells me that I've *no control.* But it is spring—late, hesitant, finicky spring.

✳

S wallows and S trawberries

THE SWINGING SIGN by the side of the road is a strawberry. All winter I pass it by without a second glance, but come the latter part of June, when the peas are not quite ready to pick and the green beans have almost broken through the ground, I start watching that sign. Then it happens. "OPEN FOR PICKING, 8:00 A.M." gets hung on the sign and I know it's time to visit Namskaket Farm, a pick-your-own strawberry farm. The sign stays up for just a few short weeks. Then it's all over for another year. An easy-to-miss, transitory experience; hesitate and the berries are gone in a wink.

On a cool, hopefully mostly cloudy day, I get to the farm around seven-fifteen, morning paper and cup of coffee on the seat beside me. About a mile down a narrow dirt road, the fields spread out. Nothing spectacular about a strawberry farm. Can't see much. There's nothing much to see from the road. I join the other cars lined up in orderly rows in the parking area, read the paper and drink my coffee. At seven-forty-five, as if by signal, we all get out and stand in line near the open-sided shed. It's very quiet. One of the attendants hands out trays on which are twelve boxes. She explains how we will be led to the particular rows that are ready for picking and tells us how to pick on the sides of the two rows we will be between. It's still very quiet. Like small schoolchildren we follow her down the rows. We put our flags in place and bend to the task.

Then I see them. Jewels. Red, ripening; small and large; tucked under leaves, riding on top. Row upon row of strawberries. The temptation is to eat breakfast right there, but the urge to pick overcomes the urge to eat. It's still very quiet. There's no yelling, no calling out to share a find of a particularly "good" plant. Even little children are strangely quiet. Some of us get right down to basics, on our hands and knees. Others bend from the waist. Every few minutes someone stands up, stretching screaming muscles. I stand and look around. The scene is otherworldly to me. Row upon row of hunched-over backs. Rounded backs, old backs, young backs. Like some old Käthe Kollwitz print of peasants in the field, the only difference is the clothing. The intensity, the mission, the sense of purpose harks back to another time. It is very quiet.

And in between the people and the plants swoop the swallows. Hundreds of swallows live in the trees surrounding the fields. Flying low over our heads like dive-bombers, they protest our intrusion. How dare we interrupt their search for insects at the precise time of day and year when the insects are the best and their young the most vociferous? Around and around they fly, launching themselves at our heads, changing direction at the last possible minute, to sail upwards, as if to gather enough momentum to try once more to dislodge us.

I am not easily dislodged. I can feel the beginning heat of a late spring day start to penetrate my shirt. The sweat trickles down my back. My mosquito spray is working overtime. I don't

stop until my twelve boxes are as full as
they can get. I place my flag where I
end my picking and make my way
between the rows back to the shed,
where my berries are weighed. These
are not cheap berries. I pay dearly for
the privilege of waking very early, working very hard in the sun, making dormant
muscles shriek and then, once home, having to
deal immediately with twelve boxes of berries.

One day I even was allowed the pleasure of going through
twice! I felt as if I had found a king's ransom with twenty-four
boxes of berries in my car. Only the next day did my body scold
me for my greed. But oh, the taste! None of that cardboard taste
of too hard berries bred to travel long distances and picked too
soon. These are mouth-watering, sun-warmed, juice-dripping
berries. They beg to be made into strawberry short cake, put into
a fruit cup, sugared and eaten as is. These berries make the best
jam. The taste is pure once-upon-a-time taste; the kind of taste
that conjures up a time when everyone went to the local farm-
stand to buy produce in season. Now we expect to find peaches in
February, fresh green beans all year and strawberries when the
snow still flies.

No more anticipation. No more trying to remember when
the first asparagus will be ready. No more are apples and oranges
the only fruit all winter.

Never mind all that. Never mind hauling loads of wood in
for the woodstove. Never mind wondering if I really do have
flesh-colored legs after looking at my navy blue long-john-clad
legs week after week. Never mind wearing so many layers of
clothes in zero-degree weather when I walk the dog that I can't

find my own outline. I know that someday soon, after the geese fly north, after the daffodils and pear trees have bloomed, after I've spread manure on the vegetable garden, then I can watch for the sign to go up. Strawberries will be ready. I can repeat my rite of spring. Once again I will bend toward the earth. I will begin again.

✳

Strawberry Jam

4 cups chopped, fresh or frozen unsweetened strawberries
3 tablespoons lemon juice
1 ½ packages powdered pectin
7 cups sugar

Combine the strawberries and lemon juice in a large nonreactive pot. Bring to a boil. Add the pectin. Return to the boil. Add the sugar slowly, stirring constantly. Bring to the boil again and boil for 1 minute, or until the jam sheets off the spoon. Pour into hot, sterilized jars. Cover with new, clean, hot lids. (See section in introduction on jar and cover preparation, pages 24–25.) Invert for 5 minutes.

Makes 7–8 eight-ounce jars

Strawberry Rhubarb Jam

I've always loved strawberry rhubarb pie. The combination of sweet strawberries and very tart rhubarb makes my mouth water as I write the words! There must be something in rhubarb that acts as a spring tonic. I can't get enough of it. This jam captures those same flavors. The rhubarb smooths out the seeds in the strawberries. The jam just slides down. It's particularly good on vanilla ice cream.

3 cups chopped, fresh or frozen unsweetened strawberries
1 cup chopped rhubarb
½ cup water
1½ packages powdered pectin
7 cups sugar

Simmer the strawberries, rhubarb and water until the rhubarb is soft, about 5 minutes. Bring to a boil. Add the pectin. Return to the boil. Add the sugar slowly, stirring constantly. Bring to the boil again and boil for 1 minute, or until the jam sheets off the spoon. Pour into hot, sterilized jars. Cover with new, clean, hot lids. (See section in introduction on jar and cover preparation, pages 24–25.) Invert for 5 minutes.

Makes 7–8 eight-ounce jars

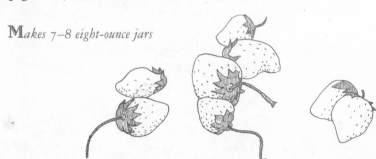

Strawberry Jam with Triple Sec Liqueur

There is just a hint of orange when you put a little triple sec liqueur in your strawberry jam. It's an unexpected, delicate taste sensation. Some friends come to the market several times each summer and load up on this jam to take to their winter home. I like this jam on homemade oatmeal bread.

4 cups chopped, fresh or frozen unsweetened strawberries
2 tablespoons lemon juice
1 ½ packages powdered pectin
8 cups sugar
⅓ cup triple sec liqueur

Put the strawberries and lemon juice in a large nonreactive pot. Bring to a boil. Add the pectin. Return to the boil. Add the sugar slowly, stirring constantly. Bring to the boil again and boil for 1 minute, or until the jam sheets off the spoon. When ready, add the triple sec and bring to the boil once more. Pour into hot, sterilized jars. Cover with new, clean, hot lids. (See section in introduction on jar and cover preparation, pages 24–25.) Invert for 5 minutes. Store in a cool place.

Makes 8–9 eight-ounce jars

Strawberry Lime Jam

Strawberry lime jam is a tropical treat. The lime takes the edge off what might otherwise be a too sweet jam. This jam came into being one day after drinking some lime seltzer water with a spoonful of strawberry jam stirred in.

4 cups chopped, fresh or frozen unsweetened strawberries
½ cup lime pulp (see Lime Marmalade, page 81)
1 ½ packages powdered pectin
7 cups sugar

Bring the strawberries and lime pulp to a boil in a large nonreactive pot. Add the pectin. Bring to the boil again. Add the sugar. Return to the boil, stirring constantly, and boil for 1 minute, or until the jam sheets off the spoon. Pour into hot, sterilized jars. Cover with new, clean, hot caps. (See section in introduction on jar and cover preparation, pages 24–25.) Invert for 5 minutes.

Makes 7–8 eight-ounce jars

Rhubarb and Ginger

WHAT AN UNEXPECTED COMBINATION of flavors. Bitter rhubarb and sweet, tangy ginger. Erica, who's British, asked me to try to make rhubarb jam. It reminds her of home. It is also very popular in India. My Indian friends tend to eat it directly out of the jar. The trick is to find good, tart rhubarb. Rhubarb that gets picked at the end of its prime growing season can become woody and tasteless.

Len and I moved a lot over the years. At first, the usual student digs. I remember moving to an apartment where I could have a garden. And a clothesline. One is as important as the other. Both made me feel that I had finally settled down.

The first plant I put into any new garden is rhubarb. I can't wait to make the first batch of rhubarb raisin sauce each spring. You can't pick rhubarb the first year. You have to wait two years before harvesting. Planting rhubarb means I'll stay put for a couple of years. Good rhubarb has large, firm stalks. The leaves of the rhubarb plant are very toxic, so keep children away, and wash your hands after you cut off the leaves. To harvest rhubarb, you pull the stems out of the plant. As the season progresses, you'll see large swelling, flowerlike stalks. Cut them off. You'll have a longer harvest.

Before winter sets in, take a basket with the bottom cut out. Place it over the whole plant, or what you can see of it. Fill the basket with good manure. The manure acts as a mulch and as protection. In the spring, the rhubarb will start to grow right up through the manure. I guess rhubarb likes a *lot* of fertilization.

Sometimes, people come to the farmers' market, bringing me rhubarb. My neighbors bring me rhubarb. I bring back jam. They don't eat rhubarb! I can't imagine *not* eating rhubarb. Rhubarb says spring.

＊

Rhubarb with Ginger Jam

The combination of rhubarb and ginger is an unexpected taste that is bittersweet and quite unusual. People who buy it once come back for it time and again.

4 cups chopped rhubarb
½ cup water
1 cup chopped preserved ginger
1½ packages powdered pectin
8 cups sugar

Simmer the rhubarb, water and ginger for about 10 minutes. This releases some of the liquid in the rhubarb and makes it easier for the jam to set. Then add the pectin, and bring the jam to a boil. If it is very thick, add no more than ½ cup of water. You have to feel the consistency of the jam when you stir. Jam that is too thick is not as appealing as jam that spoons nicely. You don't want your jam to bounce! Add the sugar slowly, stirring constantly. Return to the boil and boil for 1 minute, or until the jam sheets off the spoon. Pour into hot, sterilized jars. Cover with new, clean, hot caps. (See section in introduction on jar and cover preparation, pages 24–25.) Invert for 5 minutes.

Makes 7–8 eight-ounce jars

Raspberry Rhubarb Jam

At first, even some of my more daring jam tasters were a bit leery of this combination. I was sure they would like it. I was right! Rhubarb is a spring fruit. Soon it's gone. I chop up pounds and pounds of rhubarb and freeze it. The faithful get rewarded late into the fall with jars of this unusual jam.

3 cups whole, fresh or frozen unsweetened raspberries
1 cup chopped rhubarb
2 tablespoons lemon juice
1½ packages powdered pectin
8 cups sugar

Rhubarb contains a lot of water. Before adding anything, simmer the raspberries and the rhubarb for 5 minutes, to allow the rhubarb to give up some of the liquid. Then add the lemon juice and pectin. Bring to a boil. Add the sugar slowly, stirring constantly. Return to the boil and boil for 1 minute, or until the jam sheets off the spoon. Pour into hot, sterilized jars. Cover with new, clean, hot lids. (See section in introduction on jar and cover preparation, pages 24–25.) Invert for 5 minutes. Store in a cool place.

Makes 8–9 eight-ounce jars

Summer

Summer Is a-Comin' In

IF FALL TIPTOES IN, winter stays too long, and spring is ephemeral, there is absolutely nothing tentative about ripe, zealous summer. It takes time for the body to get used to 60-degree temperatures one day and 80-degree temperatures the next. Garden chores, which were easy in the cool spring mornings, are hard when the humidity rises so swiftly. Envelope flaps stick together, mildew appears in the most unlikely places like inside shoes, and once again I am reminded I live in an ocean environment.

There are folks who say we have only three seasons—summer, fall and winter. Summer is the one we all look forward to with a combination of delight and gritty determination. Like getting ready for an invasion, we hoard staples for the whole summer—toilet paper, detergent, anything that won't spoil and will decrease the time spent on the road or in the markets. We rehearse the routes that will take us over back roads and around the bottlenecks. We automatically add twenty minutes to any trip, and we take a deep breath. Summer arrives.

Farmers' markets . . . Green head flies biting the Most Tender Spots . . . Dinners alfresco . . . Soaking up the sun on a pristine

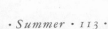

white beach . . . Zucchini plants gone wild . . . Tourists . . . Tomatoes, eggplants and peppers on the counter waiting for the foray into sauces, hot jalapeño jam and ratatouille. Baskets of basil leaves ready to turn into pesto . . . Tourists . . . Sunflowers . . . Goldfinches nesting and reproducing when the sunflower seedpods are ripe in late summer . . . Lithe, tanned grandchildren body surfing, catching the azure blue waves . . . Smaller grandchildren testing the waters for the first time . . . Bumper-to-bumper traffic on cloudy days . . . The best fried clams and lobsters "in the rough" at Moby Dick's on Route 6 in Wellfleet . . . Lilies . . . Butterflies gathering nectar on the buddleia bush . . . Hummingbirds on the impatiens . . . Sweet corn dripping with butter . . . Tomatoes . . . Bumper-to-bumper-to-bumper traffic . . . Summer repertory theater on the pier . . . Chamber music everywhere . . . Pops concerts in the park . . . Windsurfers . . . Sailboats racing back and forth across the bay . . . Digging clams at low tide . . . building fiddler crab motels in the sand when the tide goes out at the bay . . . Tasting salty tears, remembering setting sail from that bay, when the tide was right, the wind was right and the time was right . . . Sunbathing on the deck, luxuriating in the hot sun, soaking up enough to last through the winter . . . Six A.M. swims in the pond . . . Eight P.M. swims in the pond . . . Elderberries, blueberries, peaches, apricots . . . Fruitflies . . . Cucumbers in brine waiting to become bread-and-butter pickles . . . Cherry tomatoes drying in the oven, becoming "sun-dried" tomatoes . . . Green tomatoes perfect for relish and chutney . . . Hundreds and hundreds and hundreds of jars of jam . . . Boxes and boxes of peaches, pears and apricots ripening on the screened-in porch . . . Selling jam at the farmers' market . . . Hawks circling overhead, screaming their joy at a good updraft . . . A bald eagle sitting on a tree in the marsh . . . A fox drinking at the mist-shrouded pond in the early morning light . . . Playing the cello in the pit for a summer stock musical . . . Steamer clams, clam chowder, oysters on the half shell . . . Sea clams ready to be chopped and frozen for pasta and clam sauce some cold wintry night.

Lush, redolent summer.

Kritty

KRITTY SETS UP her herb, flower and houseplant stand next to my jam stand at the market. Kritty is sturdy. Her hair curls around her face. She's tan in February from working in her greenhouses in the sun and brown in summer from gardening outside. Her shoulders are broad, her hands earthworn the way a good gardener's hands should be.

We barter. One year it was jars of jam for plants. Another year I helped staff an auxiliary greenhouse for plants. And another year chutney for peaches was a good exchange. Kritty's family is the transplants and cuttings that grow and thrive under her able fingers. I know what she means when she tells me that she's happiest working quietly alone in her greenhouse or garden.

Kritty has an unpredictable peach tree. Some years it produces very well, well enough that even the loss of some peaches to marauding raccoons is not a catastrophe. Some years the peaches are small and sparse. No matter the harvest, I get peaches from Kritty. Each jar of jam made from these peaches is a treasure, hard to part with. Last year I planted peach trees. Someday I'll give Kritty jam made from my peaches.

When late fall comes, the market closes. Kritty and I reluctantly take off our sandals, put on shoes, start taking our showers indoors instead of under the blue sky, dig out our skirts and get ready to sing in the church choir. Kritty's soprano voice helps me remember hot summer days at the farmers' market.

Peach Jam from Kritty's Tree

4 cups peeled, pitted and chopped peaches
2 tablespoons lemon juice
1 ½ packages powdered pectin
7 cups sugar

Cook the peaches and lemon juice in a large nonreactive pot, until they come to a boil. Add the pectin. Return to the boil. Add the sugar slowly, stirring constantly. Bring to the boil again and boil for 1 minute, or until the jam sheets off the spoon. Pour into hot, sterilized jars. Cover with new, clean, hot caps. (See section in introduction on jar and cover preparation, pages 24–25.) Invert for 5 minutes.

Makes 7–8 eight-ounce jars

This is a basic peach recipe. For a delicious treat, try adding *any* of the following to 4 cups of peach jam:

½ cup chopped preserved ginger
½ cup lime pulp (see Lime Marmalade recipe, page 81)
⅓ cup brandy (added at the last minute)

Allow the peach mixture to come to the boil again. Pour into hot, sterilized jars. Cover with new, clean, hot caps. (See section in introduction on jar and cover preparation, pages 24–25). Invert for 5 minutes.

Makes 7–8 eight-ounce jars

Peach with Brandy Jam

One day, while searching the aisles of my favorite liquor store for some new and unusual liqueurs to add to jam, I spied a bottle of brandy. It was a fortuitous find. Brandy adds sophistication to the ordinary. It conjures up wood-paneled libraries, overstuffed chairs and "important" talk.

4 cups peeled, pitted, and chopped peaches
2 tablespoons lemon juice
1 1/2 packages powdered pectin
8 cups sugar
1/3 cup good-quality brandy

Put the peaches and lemon juice in a large nonreactive pot. Bring to a boil. Add the pectin. Return to the boil. Add the sugar slowly, stirring constantly. Bring to the boil again and boil for 1 minute, or until the jam sheets off the spoon. Add the brandy. When ready, pour into hot, sterilized jars. Cover with new, clean, hot caps. (See section in introduction on jar and cover preparation, pages 24–25.) Invert for 5 minutes. Store in a cool place.

Makes 8–9 eight-ounce jars

Ginger Peach Marmalade

One day I was looking at different kinds of marmalade in a "gourmet" food store. I noticed a jar of ginger peach marmalade. I can do that, I said to myself. It took a few attempts to get the ratio of oranges to peaches just right. The resulting marmalade is a breath of summer tinged with a hint of autumn. One of my customers uses this jam as a glaze when she broils chicken. She's right. It tastes wonderful!

6–8 large peaches, pitted and peeled
2 large oranges, unpeeled and cut into sections, with seeds removed
½ cup chopped preserved ginger
½–1 cup water
1 package powdered pectin
8 cups sugar

Into a food processor fitted with the cutting blade, chop the peaches, oranges and ginger until they are a fine pulp. You should have 4 cups of fruit to work with. Put the mixture into a large nonreactive pot with water, the amount of which depends on the thickness of the fruit. Simmer for 10 minutes on a very low heat. Then bring to a boil, and add the pectin. Bring to the boil again and add the sugar, stirring constantly.

Cook on low heat, stirring constantly, allowing the marmalade to bubble a little, for approximately 10 minutes. At that time, place a spoonful of jam on a cold plate in the refrigerator. If in 10 minutes it has developed a skin, it is ready. If not, keep cooking, and try again in a few minutes.

When ready, pour into hot, sterilized jars. Cover with new, clean, hot caps. (See section in introduction on jar and cover preparation, pages 24–25.) Invert for 5 minutes.

Makes 7–8 eight-ounce jars

The combination of peach, ginger and orange is irresistible. My favorite way to have this is on bran muffins, but I've been known to put it on vanilla ice cream and even eat it straight out of the jar.

Pear with Ginger Jam

Pears are a most perfect fruit. They ripen slowly and evenly. Some pear lovers (I'm one) eat them when they are not quite ripe and are still crunchy. You can tell when they are ripe; they turn color slowly, giving you ample time to decide what to do with them. My favorite thing to do with just-right pears is to make pear with ginger jam. The sweet smoothness of pears, combined with the tongue-curling smartness of the ginger, is a surprise. The trick is to use just the right amount of ginger; too much and you'll kill the jam.

The first jar of jam I ever gave a local market to try was pear with ginger. One of the managers took it home to taste. Her son ate the whole jar, plain. No toast, no crackers . . . straight out of the jar. I'm grateful to that boy. Use almost-ripe Bartlett or Anjou pears.

4 cups chopped Bartlett or Anjou pear pulp (see page 23)
½ cup chopped preserved ginger
2 tablespoons lemon juice
1½ packages powdered pectin
7 cups sugar

Put the pear pulp, ginger and lemon juice in a large nonreactive pot. Bring to a boil. Add the pectin. Return to the boil. Add the sugar slowly, stirring constantly. Boil for 1 minute, or until the jam sheets off the spoon. Pour into hot, sterilized jars. Cover with new, clean, hot caps. (See section in introduction on jar and cover preparation, pages 24–25.) Invert for 5 minutes.

Makes 7–8 eight-ounce jars

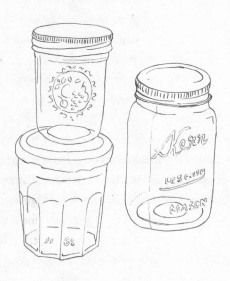

Pear with Frangelico Jam

Frangelico is a hazelnut liqueur. It has a wonderful nutty flavor that goes particularly well with pears. The combination is subtle and very smooth. People giggle when they ask me if they'll get a kick from eating jam with liqueur. Unfortunately, no. The alcohol burns off in the cooking. What's left is the flavor. I don't sell a lot of this jam, but those in the know—those who know what frangelico is—light up when they see it.

4 cups chopped Bartlett or Anjou pear pulp (see page 23)
2 tablespoons lemon juice
1 1/2 packages powdered pectin
7 cups sugar
1/3 cup frangelico

Put the pear pulp and lemon juice in a large nonreactive pot. Bring to a boil. Add the pectin. Return to the boil. Add the sugar slowly, stirring constantly. When the mixture begins to boil, add the frangelico. Bring to the boil again and boil for 1 minute, or until the jam sheets off the spoon. Pour into hot, sterilized jars. Cover with new, clean, hot caps. (See section in introduction on jar and cover preparation, pages 24–25.) Invert for 5 minutes.

Makes 7–8 eight-ounce jars

Absolutely Aromatic Apricot Jam

Like peaches, apricots make wonderful jam. I suppose if I lived in the Northwest, where apricots are plentiful, they wouldn't seem so special. Here in the East, the apricot season is a short one. I buy many boxes at one time. I spread the apricots in a single layer in a large box. Sometimes, one small bruised spot can spread, causing any fruit touching the affected one to also become rotten. Spreading them in a single layer with lots of space in between each piece of fruit prevents this bruising. When they are a little soft to the touch, I wash them, pit them and chop them in my food processor. Apricot skins are tight, so I leave them on. A little texture is nice. Then I transfer the pulp to quart bags and freeze them, taking out only the amount I need for each batch.

You can combine apricots with rum, brandy, lime, oranges or ginger. Be careful when you make apricot orange jam. Too strong an orange flavor will mask the delicate taste of the apricots.

4 cups unpeeled, pitted and chopped apricots
2 tablespoons lemon juice
1 ½ packages powdered pectin
7 cups sugar

Combine the apricots and lemon juice in a large nonreactive pot. Bring to a boil. Add the pectin. Return to the boil. Add the sugar slowly, stirring constantly. Apricots tend to stick to the bottom of the pot, so you have to be vigilant. Bring to the boil again and boil for 1 minute. Skim off any foam. Pour into hot, sterilized jars. Cover with new, clean, hot caps. (See section in introduction on jar and cover preparation, pages 24–25.) Invert for 5 minutes.

Makes 7–8 eight-ounce jars

Next to my new peach trees are two new apricot trees. They're rather spindly now. Last year I had one ripe apricot. I was delighted! So was my resident chipmunk. He ate it. Someday I'll be able to label some jars Absolutely Aromatic Apricot Jam from Joan's Tree.

Apricot with Rum Jam

I like to think that some pirate ship traveling the South Seas came upon some apricots, and in order to preserve them, the captain packed them in rum. It's a nice thought. Apricot with rum jam is almost as good as a trip to far-off tropical lands.

4 cups pitted and chopped apricots, with skins left on
2 tablespoons lemon juice
1 ½ packages powdered pectin
8 cups sugar
⅓ cup dark or light rum

Put the apricots and lemon juice in a large nonreactive pot. Bring to a boil. Add the pectin. Return to the boil. Add the sugar slowly, stirring constantly. Bring to the boil again and boil for 1 minute, or until the jam sheets off the spoon. Add the rum. Bring back to the boil. Pour into hot, sterilized jars. Cover with new, clean, hot caps. (See section in introduction on jar and cover preparation, pages 24–25.) Invert for 5 minutes. Store in a cool place.

Makes 8–9 eight-ounce jars

Apricot with Lime Jam

Did you ever sit at a drugstore soda fountain and ask for a lime rickey? Adding lime to jam gives the jam that extra tang that reminds me of that cool drink. Try lime with raspberry and peach jam as well as apricot. You'll not be disappointed.

4 cups pitted and chopped apricots
⅓ cup lime pulp
1½ packages powdered pectin
8 cups sugar

Put apricots and lime pulp in a large nonreactive pot. Bring to a boil. Add the pectin. Return to the boil. Add the sugar slowly, stirring constantly. Bring to the boil again and boil for 1 minute, or until the jam sheets off the spoon. Pour into hot, sterilized jars. Cover with new, clean, hot caps. (See section in introduction on jar and cover preparation, pages 24–25.) Invert for 5 minutes. Store in a cool place.

Makes 8–9 eight-ounce jars

Jalapeño Pepper Jam

The requests for this jam start as soon as the farmers' market opens in the spring. My pepper plants are in as soon as the nights stay above 50 degrees, since peppers do not do well when it's cool. Then I anxiously watch to see if they blossom and fruit. I mulch the plants with straw to keep the weeds out and the moisture in the soil, and assure my pepper jam addicts that there will be ample jam this year. Jalapeño jam, mixed with a little cream cheese spread on a cracker, is a gourmet hors d'oeuvre. The jam is hot; the cream cheese cool; the color like a Christmas ornament. Truly, a special jam. Just remember to wear rubber or latex gloves when working with jalapeño peppers. The juice is powerful and can cause a lot of pain if you accidentally rub your face or eyes. Slice the peppers and remove the seeds.

4 cups, finely chopped jalapeño peppers
1 sweet red pepper, chopped
1 can unreconstituted frozen apple juice
2 tablespoons lemon juice
1½ packages powdered pectin
8 cups sugar

Combine the peppers, apple juice and lemon juice in a large non-reactive pot. Bring to a boil. Add the pectin. Return to the boil. Add the sugar slowly, stirring constantly. Bring to the boil again and boil for 1 minute, or until the jam sheets off the spoon. Pour into hot, sterilized jars. Cover with new, clean, hot caps. (See section in introduction on jar and cover preparation, pages 24–25.) Invert for 5 minutes. You'll find that the peppers tend to float to the top, so as the jam continues to firm up, gently shake each jar to redistribute the peppers. As the jam jells, the pepper pieces will stay suspended throughout the jar. Store in a cool place.

Makes 8–9 eight-ounce jars

Pineapple Ginger Jam

One day I made some pineapple chutney. The combination of pineapple, spices and ginger was irresistible. I decided to try pineapple ginger jam. While not a rousing success, those who like both ingredients tell me that the combination of the hot and sweet is just right. I think it's wonderful spread on French toast. But I always did like pineapple.

4 cups canned crushed pineapple, drained
½ cup chopped preserved ginger
2 tablespoons lemon juice
1½ packages powdered pectin
7–8 cups sugar, to taste

Combine the pineapple, ginger and lemon juice in a large nonreactive pot. Bring to a boil. Add the pectin. Return to the boil. Add the sugar slowly, stirring constantly. Bring to the boil again and boil for 1 minute, or until the jam sheets off the spoon. Pour into hot, sterilized jars. Cover with new, clean, hot lids. (See section in introduction on jar and cover preparation, pages 24–25.) Invert for 5 minutes. Store in a cool place.

Makes 7–8 eight-ounce jars

Old Lady Keough
and the Blackberries

WE CALLED HER OLD LADY KEOUGH. I can't tell you what "old" meant. She could have been forty and "old" to me. I never did meet or see her. Just her reputation relayed with gusto by my older sisters was enough to strike fear in my five-year-old heart. I can't even tell you whether her so-called reputation as a mean woman with a really mean dog was warranted. The dog was a husky with dichromatic eyes, a fact my sisters impressed upon me as representing evil. I was not only dutifully impressed, I think I was breathless every time I walked through that field.

Old Lady Keough lived in Fiskdale, then a tiny town in central Massachusetts close enough to Worcester for my father, who was a loom designer, to commute to work. Too small to be on most maps, Fiskdale is also the town where Big Alum Lake is. Ms. Keough owned our cottage and many other properties in the area. We had to walk through her fields to get to the penny candy store and post office, one and the same. Blackberries grew in tumbled abundance in the field. These blackberries were probably the first wild fruit I ever picked. It must have been a powerful experience. The memory of those days has stayed with me all these years.

My family went to Big Alum Lake every summer. The lake is a natural volcanic kettle pond, named for the alum suspended in the water. There were no mosquitoes. The alum healed cuts and scratches. The pond water was so clear that we could sit in our dining room and still see the bottom of the pond, yards and yards away. We spent many hours diving for the glittering little amethysts that littered the pond bottom.

We arrived the day after school let out and came home the day before school started. Our cottage, once an ice cream stand, was tiny—so tiny that we could lean against the house and hang our legs over the railing.

It's funny what you can remember. I vividly remember that cottage—two bedrooms, a small living room, tiny kitchen, a dining room two steps up from the kitchen and the porch. Somehow, five of us managed to fit in. We never seemed to mind the close quarters, although I must admit I wasn't thrilled when my sisters came into the room where I slept and teased me with jars filled with katydids, winged bugs that make a loud scritch-scratch noise when they rub their legs together.

There was no running water. My dad dug a well. At night we kept a full pitcher of water in the kitchen to prime the pump in the morning. The sounds of water gurgling up from deep within the well and the rich smell of coffee brewing woke me each morning.

There was no indoor plumbing. The outhouse, cheerfully

called the Castle on the Hill, perched at the top of the hill behind the house. Little did we know about effluent flow and plume direction, or that you don't dig a well downstream from an outhouse!

I didn't like that outhouse one bit. I hated going up there alone and refused to go after dark. We had a chamber pot, very cold to the touch, to use in the middle of the night. Consequently, my mattress spent many days drying out over the railing, a source of great embarrassment to my five-year-old soul.

We lived in our bathing suits and would go for a dip every morning before breakfast. It wasn't easy to jump into that crystal-clear, cold water at that early hour. The rewards were great. Waiting for us as we dashed back to the cottage were grapefruit halves sprinkled with confectioners' sugar and hot cinnamon toast.

After breakfast we frequently walked to the penny candy store. Now, I know that the walk couldn't have been too long, since we would always be back in time for a swim before lunch. But I was a small child. The walk seemed interminable. Hot and tired almost as soon as we set out, I had to hurry to keep up with the older girls, to make sure I'd get my share of Penuche fudge. The horror of falling behind and coming face-to-face with either Ms. Keough or her dog kept my pace brisk.

But the anticipation of blackberry cobbler, made sweeter by blackberries snatched from Ms. Keough's fields on the way back from the penny candy store, really motivated me. Fortunately, we always escaped Old Lady Keough and her dog, and when we got home with the juicy blackberries we'd managed not to eat, my mother would make cobbler. Bubbling and sweet, it was a rich reward for our endeavors. How we savored that dessert!

We handled those blackberries carefully. I handle handpicked blackberries just as carefully now. I gently nudge them from their brambles, plucking them where they are attached to their stems. I look for berries that are not quite ripe, since these will make better jam. I just eat the really ripe ones as I pick. Lunch to go! When I get home, I try to make jam as soon as possible, because ripe blackberries don't last too long.

I live on a pond now. I can walk down my driveway, cross the street and be there. I love to slip into the water, silent as an otter, before breakfast, when the mist is rising from the pond surface. There are no amethysts on the bottom. There are no blackberries. There is no alum. I go home . . . . grapefruit and cinnamon toast. Curious what you take with you through life.

Blackberry with Lime Jam

4 cups chopped, fresh or frozen unsweetened blackberries
¾ cup lime pulp (see Lime Marmalade recipe, page 81)
1 ½ packages powdered pectin
7 cups sugar

Combine the blackberries and lime in a large nonreactive pot. Bring to a boil. Add the pectin. Return to the boil. Slowly add the sugar, stirring constantly. Bring to the boil again. Cook until the fruit sheets off the spoon. Pour into hot, sterilized jars. Screw on new, clean, hot lids. (See section in introduction on jar and cover preparation, pages 24–25.) Invert for 5 minutes.

Makes 7–8 eight-ounce jars

If you want to, you can leave out the lime. The lime adds a subtle but distinct tang. You can cook the blackberries with water to cover, and, when soft, put them through a Foley Food Mill to get out most of the seeds. The resulting jam I call Almost Seedless Blackberry Jam. People with dentures understand. They buy it right up. I also use blackberries in combination with other fruits, such as raspberries and strawberries, or with liqueurs. Blackberries are very versatile. Plain blackberry jam is also wonderful. I just like to experiment. Old Lady Keough would approve.

Blackberry with Brandy Jam

4 cups chopped, fresh or frozen unsweetened blackberries
2 tablespoons lemon juice
1 ½ packages powdered pectin
7–8 cups sugar
⅓ cup good-quality brandy

Combine the blackberries and lemon juice in a large nonreactive pot. Bring to a boil. Add the pectin. Return to the boil. Add the sugar slowly, stirring constantly. Bring to the boil again and boil for 1 minute. Add the brandy and continue to boil for 1 more minute, or until the jam sheets off the spoon. Pour into hot, sterilized jars. Cover with new, clean, hot caps. (See section in introduction on jar and cover preparation, pages 24–25.) Invert for 5 minutes.

Makes 7–8 eight-ounce jars

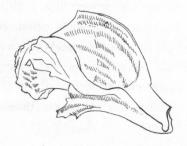

Marty Andersen Really Knew His Berries

Marty Andersen died three years ago. I read about it in the paper. He had been in a nursing home for two years after experiencing several strokes. I had gone to visit him, talking softly, reminding him of long-ago days in the berry patch. No longer able to speak, he could only rub my arm and say, "No, no, no." My longtime neighbor, superb artist, remarkable pianist, gardener extraordinaire, apple pie and bread baker, he was the embodiment of what every Grandpa should be, his inner light shining through his bright blue eyes and smiling sweet face.

We met in 1959. The ad in the paper at home had advertised a summer cottage near the beach for $85 a week. Our family went for one week the first summer, two weeks the second and three weeks for the next nine years. By then, our family had grown to five children and was too much for his little unheated, primitive place. We bought land, built our own cottage, bought another piece of land and eventually built a year-round home, all on the same street. My family had a thirty-five-year love affair with the marsh, the herons, the clams and Marty.

I miss him most in the summer, when it's berry-picking time. For Marty Andersen really knew his berries. Mostly, he knew every glacial kettle, every field, every little dirt path that led to the wild blueberry and blackberry patches—even to the cemetery, long since abandoned, where on a south-facing slope grew the largest, roundest, bluest berries.

"You have to pick berries before the sun climbs too high in the sky," Marty would say as we piled out of our car. "Tuck your socks into your pants legs," he warned.

"And spray well. The ticks are bad and the mosquitoes worse," and solemn little faces listened and bent in unison, following his example. Then armed with the coffee can buckets he had made, we marched down the steep slope into the glacial kettle, each step permanently etched in our minds.

"One for the bucket and one for the mouth" is the universal axiom when picking blueberries. Giddy with such unexpected profusion, the children ate their way. However, with my children, the spirit of competition won out and soon they picked berries as fast as they could, to see who would be the first to scramble back up the slope to dump the contents of their can in the huge washtub that Marty had in the back of his truck. "Over here," someone would yell when they'd spot another loaded bush. Off they would all flutter like bright butterflies, responding to that ageless imperative to "have enough." They rarely shared their treasures.

Picking joy is short-lived, about three coffee cans full. By 9:30 A.M., Marty was ready to pack up and head for the kitchen, but not before he had checked little tongues to make sure they were blue enough. Back home, it was inspection time for ticks and a wash with Fels Naphtha Soap to prevent poison ivy. The berries were picked over; the leaves and green berries, of which there were many, thrown out; and the berries packed into bags for the freezer or into the pot for a childhood favorite, stewed blueberries. Only when the stewed blueberries had been added to cold milk, turning it a brilliant blue, did the children run off to embark on another adventure with Marty, perhaps to the mud flats, where he taught them to dig razor clams with their hands, identify good oysters and quahogs, or observe the prehistoric mating rituals of horseshoe crabs.

My children are all grown. Houses now line the road to the kettle and most of the blueberry bushes have been bulldozed under in the name of progress. I've found new places to pick blueberries, huckleberries and blackberries. I teach my grandchildren to tuck their socks into their pants. I check their tongues to make sure they are blue enough. All the necessary things one must do to perpetuate the memory of Marty Andersen; to do all the things that sun-drenched summers on Cape Cod dictate. Now, when we come home with our treasures, the children know that they will go home with jam. Marty didn't teach me to make jam. But every time I bend to pick a berry, every time I make a jar of wild blueberry or blackberry jam, I capture the sun of summer. I capture, for a few brief moments, Marty Andersen's smile. I smile in remembrance.

✷

Blueberry Jam

4 cups chopped blueberries
3 tablespoons lemon juice
½ cup water
1½ packages powdered pectin
8 cups sugar

Combine the chopped blueberries, lemon juice and water in a large nonreactive pot. Bring to a boil. Add the pectin. Return to the boil. Slowly add the sugar, stirring constantly to prevent scorching. Bring to the boil again and boil for 1 minute, or until the jam sheets off the spoon. Fill hot, sterilized jars. Cover with new, clean, hot lids. (See section in introduction on jar and cover preparation, pages 24–25.) Invert for 5 minutes.

Makes *7–8 eight-ounce jars*

Blueberry Rhubarb Jam

This may sound like an odd combination. Sometimes, my creativity gets the best of me. I'll try a small batch of something new, test-market it and wait for reactions. This jam has proven to be a winner. The combination of tart rhubarb and sweet blueberry makes it just right.

3 cups chopped blueberries
1 cup chopped rhubarb
½ cup water
1½ packages powdered pectin
7 cups sugar

Put the blueberries, rhubarb and water in a large nonreactive pot. Simmer until soft, about 10 minutes. Make sure the fruit does not scorch. Add a little water, if necessary. When the fruit is soft, bring to a boil. Add the pectin. Return to the boil. Slowly add the sugar, stirring constantly. Bring to the boil again and boil for 1 minute, or until the jam sheets off the spoon. Pour into hot, sterilized jars. Cover with new, clean, hot caps. (See section in introduction on jar and cover preparation, pages 24–25.) Invert for 5 minutes.

Makes 7–8 eight-ounce jars

Three-Fruit Jam

This jam combines three of my favorite fruits in a wonderful mélange. Occasionally, the jam does not jell. I can't give you any rational explanation. The jam goddess is not with me is as good a reason as any. In any event, this jam tastes wonderful on pancakes. I sell not-quite-thick-enough jam as Pancake Sauce.

2 cups chopped, fresh or frozen unsweetened blueberries
2 cups chopped, fresh or frozen unsweetened blackberries
2 cups chopped, fresh or frozen unsweetened strawberries
½ cup water
3 tablespoons lemon juice
1½ packages powdered pectin
10 cups sugar

Put all the fruit, water and lemon juice in a large nonreactive pot. Simmer for about 5 minutes, or just enough to slightly soften the fruit. Bring the fruit to a boil. Add the pectin. Return to the boil. Slowly add the sugar, stirring constantly. Cook until the jam sheets off the spoon. Pour into hot, sterilized jars. Cover with new, clean, hot caps. (See section in introduction on jar and cover preparation, pages 24–25.) Invert for 5 minutes.

Makes 9–10 eight-ounce jars

To enlarge this recipe, use:

8 cups fruit
1 cup water
3 tablespoons lemon juice
3 packages powdered pectin
13 cups sugar

Proceed as you usually would. It's just as easy to make 17 jars of jam as it is to make 9! And you'll always have some extra to give away as gifts.

Makes 17–18 eight-ounce jars

Four-Fruit Jam

You'll never have to worry about pleasing the most demanding tastes if you make four-fruit jam. The name alone conjures up hot meadows, gnats buzzing around your head, cold lemonade. This jam combines all the best of summer.

2 cups chopped, fresh or frozen unsweetened raspberries
2 cups chopped, fresh or frozen unsweetened strawberries
2 cups chopped, fresh or frozen unsweetened blackberries
2 cups chopped, fresh or frozen unsweetened blueberries
3 tablespoons lemon juice
3 packages powdered pectin
12 cups sugar

Put all the fruit and the lemon juice in a large nonreactive pot. Bring to a boil. Add the pectin. Return to the boil. Add the sugar slowly, stirring constantly. Bring to the boil again and boil for 1 minute, or until the jam sheets off the spoon. Pour into hot, sterilized jars. Cover with new, clean, hot caps. (See section in introduction on jar and cover preparation, pages 24–25.) Invert for 5 minutes. Store in a cool place.

Makes 18–20 eight-ounce jars

If you want to make half this recipe, just use 1 cup each of the fruit, half the amount of pectin, a little less lemon juice and 8 cups of sugar.

Alice Hiscock

THERE ARE SOME DISTINCT REWARDS associated with sitting at the farmers' market week after week—new friendships; a devoted and loyal clientele; the sweetest vegetables; flowers picked in the predawn cool; the freshest clams and oysters, still shimmering with bay water; cooking lessons; rediscovering old friends and even making some money. If you're a people watcher as I am, working for several hours, sometimes in the sun, doesn't seem too onerous.

That's how I first noticed Alice Hiscock as she walked through the market. Very small, bent over, hair in a bun, with Keds sneakers and denim skirt, she had a curious, alert face. She appeared sturdy.

One day she approached me. "Would you like some red currants?" That's like asking a jam maker if she would like to go to berry heaven! "I'll bring you some next week." She decided that $1 a pound would be sufficient.

The next week she was back. "I've only got five pounds. Next week I'll bring you five more and that will be the end of them. The heat made them ripen all at once."

She came back with more tiny round jewels and that's when I bent way over and kissed the top of her head. Alice told me that she was eighty-six, had slowed down some and had given up three of her biggest gardens. Now she managed to take care of only one vegetable garden, all her flower beds, her fruit trees and her berry plants. Only!

I took the currants and made jars and jars of the most spectacular scarlet jam. My crown jewels. I saved a few jars for Alice and reluctantly sold all the rest in one week. I doubt if I will ever see a currant without remembering Alice Hiscock.

I suspect that someday I'll be eighty-six. I hope I can grow old with as much vitality, curiosity and determination as Alice. I'll pick berries, tend my gardens, maybe even make jam, swim in the surf; reminded that being is a blessing.

※

Red Currant Jam

Cover washed currants with water, about 1 inch above the top of the currants. Cook slowly until soft. This won't take very long. Put through a Foley Food Mill. The seeds and skins will be left behind.

4 cups currant pulp and juice
2 tablespoons lemon juice
1 ½ packages powdered pectin
8 cups sugar

Put the currants and lemon juice in a large nonreactive pot. Bring to a boil. Add the pectin. Return to the boil. Add the sugar slowly, stirring constantly. Bring to the boil again and boil for 1 minute, or until the jam sheets off the spoon. Pour into hot, sterilized jars. Cover with new, clean, hot caps. (See section in introduction on jar and cover preparation, pages 24–25.) Invert for 5 minutes.

Makes 7–8 eight-ounce jars

Regal Royal Raspberries

EVERY ONCE IN A WHILE someone will tell me about his or her raspberry patch. "I've got more than I could ever use. If you want some, just call and let me know if you'd like to come pick. I'm sure you could get a quart or two." A quart or two! Little do they know that they are talking to a raspberry addict. I've grown my own, but never have had enough for jam. I tend to eat them as they ripen. I think I'd need an acre of raspberries to have enough for one week's production.

Raspberries are the tenderest of fruit. Not only do they bruise easily, they don't keep too long after picking, either because they spoil or because I have an irresistible urge to eat them right away. Sometimes my handpicked berries don't even make it to the kitchen, as they really are the most delectable eaten right off the vine, after they've been baking in the hot afternoon sun. Raspberry plants have brambles that deter all but the most persistent picker, provide birds with breakfast fit for a king, and require diligence in planting, pruning and maintaining.

I buy individually frozen, whole, unsweetened raspberries, fifty pounds at a time. I don't always have the luxury of picking all my own fruit, one of the drawbacks of an expanding business. I do have the luxury of trying out all kinds of raspberry jam combinations.

My primitive marketing research tells me that anything with raspberries sells well—so well, that one day I received a call from a man who said to me, "You have the next-to-best raspberry jam in the world." Laughingly, I asked him where the best was. He mentioned some shop in Paris and asked if I'd ever been there, a strange question for an overworked jam maker. The next week he drove for four hours to come buy a case of raspberry jam!

I may not be in Paris, but my raspberry jam is as good as it gets. Yours will be, too, if you remember to use enough fruit and not too much sugar. I still go pick "a quart or two." It keeps me connected to the earth and to my friends who are interested in my success.

Parisian Raspberry Jam

4 cups whole, fresh or frozen unsweetened raspberries
3 tablespoons lemon juice
1 ½ packages powdered pectin
8 cups sugar

Put the raspberries and lemon juice in a large nonreactive pot.
Bring to a boil. Add the pectin. Return to the boil. Add the sugar
slowly, stirring constantly. Bring to the boil again and boil for
1 minute, or until the jam sheets off the spoon. When ready, pour
into hot, sterilized jars. Cover with new, clean, hot caps. (See section in introduction on jar and cover preparation, pages 24–25.)
Invert for 5 minutes.

Makes 7–8 eight-ounce jars

Raspberry Rum Jam

This jam is one of the most popular. It's an instant sellout at the local farmers' market, where every Saturday hoards of people come to buy fresh and processed foods, locally grown and produced. The atmosphere is carnival and corner country store all rolled into one. Flowers and herbs; greens and vegetables; eggs and shellfish. Jam and baked goods. Breakfast, lunch and dinner, bought as you stroll around.

4 cups whole, fresh or frozen unsweetened raspberries
2 tablespoons lemon juice
1 ½ packages powdered pectin
7 cups sugar
⅓ cup rum

Combine the raspberries and lemon juice in a heavy nonreactive pot. Bring to a boil. Add the pectin. Return to the boil. Add the sugar, stirring constantly. When the jam sheets off the spoon, add the rum, and boil for another minute or so, making sure that the jam still sheets off the spoon. Pour into hot, sterilized jars. Cover with new, clean, hot lids. (See section in introduction on jar and cover preparation, pages 24–25.) Invert for 5 minutes.

Makes 7–8 eight-ounce jars

Raspberry Peach Jam

1 cup whole, fresh or frozen, unsweetened raspberries
3 cups peeled, pitted and chopped peaches
3 tablespoons lemon juice
1½ packages powdered pectin
7 cups sugar

Combine the raspberries, peaches and lemon juice in a large non-reactive pot. Bring to a boil. Add the pectin. Return to the boil. Slowly add the sugar, stirring constantly. When the jam sheets off the spoon, pour into hot, sterilized jars. Cover with new, clean, hot lids. (See section in introduction on jar and cover preparation, pages 24–25.) Invert for 5 minutes. It's important not to overdo it with the raspberries because they can overwhelm the peaches.

Makes 8–9 eight-ounce jars

I like this jam on anything—bread, crackers, ice cream, even in a glass of seltzer water. Done just right, this combination is the essence of a sun-drenched summer.

Raspberry Amaretto Jam

Amaretto is an almond-flavored liqueur. It goes very well with raspberries. This jam is a favorite with some store owners, who eat it themselves; it never does get to the counter. I always remember to put an extra jar in the box when delivering to these folks.

4 cups whole, fresh or frozen unsweetened raspberries
2 tablespoons lemon juice
1 ½ packages powdered pectin
8 cups sugar
⅓ cup amaretto

Put the raspberries and lemon juice in a large nonreactive pot. Bring to a boil. Add the pectin. Return to the boil. Add the sugar slowly, stirring constantly. Bring to the boil again and boil for 1 minute. Add the amaretto. Bring to the boil yet again. When the jam sheets off the spoon, pour into hot, sterilized jars. Cover with new, clean, hot lids. (See section in introduction on jar and cover preparation, pages 24–25.) Invert for 5 minutes. Store in a cool place.

Makes 7–8 eight-ounce jars

Nonnie and the Elderberries

MY OLDEST SON, Roger, loved Nonnie. She loved him right back. When Nonnie was very old and beginning to fade, I'd consistently have to reintroduce myself by saying, "I'm Roger's mom." "Ah," she'd respond, her face lighting up. He was part of her reality.

I remember Roger, at the age of fifteen, dressed up in the only suit he's ever owned, coming downstairs very early one morning. "I'm taking Nonnie out for breakfast." He marched out, picked her up at her house, which was very close by, and the two of them, at six-thirty in the morning, walked to the local eggs and bacon spot. Roger took her home after breakfast, came home, changed into jeans and went off to school.

Many years later Roger drove down from Vermont to be a pallbearer at her funeral. She was the only grandmother he really had. Nonnie, officially Helen Chrisman, was the mother of one of my very best friends, and had vitality, spirit, humor, determination and a contagious laugh—all intact at the age of eighty, even at eighty-five. That was the summer she refused a perfectly good bed in my house and slept on a mat in a tent in my yard. That was the summer she went swimming in the bracing, probably

57-degree Atlantic Ocean, laughing as she marched into the roiling surf. I held my breath. *She* laughed as she was swept back onto the beach.

Nonnie taught me everything I know about elderberries. I've been told, on good authority, that Nonnie always traveled with a "loot bag," just in case you "come across something good to pick along the road." So it was, one morning, when we were driving down the dirt road near the dump, looking for beach plums. "Stop the car," she yelled. "Elderberries!"

I stopped, not knowing what I was looking at. I always carry a bucket in my car, just in case. We were prepared. We marched into the damp brush. Towering above us were what, to my eyes, looked just like Virginia creeper plants with berries. Elderberries have flat, plate-sized clusters of berries that form at the ends of those long stems.

The berries are a deep, deep purple. They grow in inaccessible places, so when you find a clump the trick is to test the ground for bogginess, gauge the poison ivy risk and then . . . go for it. You don't pick elderberries individually. You cut off the whole stem, with the cluster of berries still intact. The berries are smaller than the smallest petite peas. Hundreds of berries in one cluster on one stem. Sounds like a treasure? Wait till you get that bucket filled with berries and stems home. Then the fun begins.

First all the berry heads have to be stripped off the stem.

Second all the leaves, green berries and tiny stems to which the individual berries are attached have to be removed. You need a lot of children for this chore. Once, and only once, will they think that picking over elderberries is fun. Make the most of that enthusiasm. The next time you mention elderberries, they'll disappear.

When all the elderberries, stems and detritus have been separated, put the berries in a deep pot, cover with water a couple of inches above the top of the berries and cook until they are soft.

I put the whole mass through a Foley Food Mill to get out most of the seeds, which, as you can imagine, are minute—just the kind that gets stuck between your tooth and gum, the kind you keep worrying with your tongue until you get it out.

You can make elderberry pie with the berries just as you pick them, or you can make elderberry jam. I've never seen them for sale in the market, but I do have friends who have cultivated elderberries growing in their yard. Perhaps someday I'll try a few plants in my yard.

Elderberries taste a bit like blackberries and a bit like blueberries—not quite sweet, not quite bitter. The resulting jam looks black until you hold it up to the light. It's really royal purple. The taste *is* fit for a king.

※

Elderberry Jam

4 cups elderberry pulp and juice
3 tablespoons lemon juice
1 ½ packages powdered pectin
7 cups sugar

Put the elderberry pulp and lemon juice in a large nonreactive pot. Bring to a boil. Add the pectin. Return to the boil. Add the sugar slowly, stirring constantly. Return to the boil and boil for 1 minute, or until the jam sheets off the spoon. Pour into hot, sterilized jars. Cover with new, clean, hot caps. (See section in introduction on jar and cover preparation, pages 24–25.) Invert for 5 minutes.

Makes 7–8 eight-ounce jars

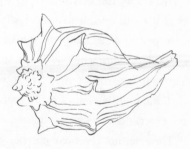

Bees, Birds and Sour Cherries

RANDY AND PAUL have an old, grand sour cherry tree in their yard. Sometimes it is fruitful, sometimes barren. I can't tell you why some years are better than others. For several years I looked longingly at those cherries, but didn't feel comfortable asking for some. One summer they told me that they had enough for their needs, and that I could pick the rest if I wanted to. I didn't need a second invitation. Disappearing into the leafy branches, I am a fairy princess in some magical storybook, surrounded by leaves and fruit, bees and birds. My only fee is a few jars of ruby red jam.

Last year the storm they called a near-miss hurricane broke off many branches. The tree is old and dying. I decided that I needed a cherry tree of my own. My tree catalog had some dwarf trees that I will be able to harvest without climbing too high. I bought one, and last fall planted it in my yard. I can see it from my laundry room window. Planting new trees gives me the incentive to take care of myself, to nourish my body as well as my soul. I want to be around many more years. I want to harvest many quarts of my own sour cherries.

These are not the sweet cherries we buy in the market to eat out of hand. These are pie cherries. I buy mine pitted and frozen, or, if I've picked my own, I sit and pit them. They are then stored in quart bags and frozen. Cherries have an elusive flavor when cooked. I generally add complementary fruit or rum.

Rum adds so much to jam! I add ⅓ cup at the very end, allow the alcohol to boil off and then process. Pineapple also works well with cherries.

❋

Cherry Pineapple Jam

3 cups pitted and chopped sour cherries
1 cup canned crushed pineapple, drained
2 tablespoons lemon juice
1 ½ packages powdered pectin
7 cups sugar

Put the cherries, pineapple and lemon juice in a large nonreactive pot. Bring to a boil. Add the pectin. Return to the boil. Add the sugar slowly, stirring constantly. Bring to the boil again and boil for 1 minute, or until the jam sheets off the spoon. Pour into hot, sterilized jars. Cover with new, clean, hot caps. (See section in introduction on jar and cover preparation, pages 24–25.) Invert for 5 minutes.

Makes 7–8 eight-ounce jars

Sour Cherry Jam

4 cups pitted and chopped sour cherries
2 tablespoons lemon juice
1 ½ packages powdered pectin
7–8 cups sugar

Put the cherries and lemon juice in a large nonreactive pot. Bring to a boil. Add the pectin. Return to the boil. Add the sugar slowly, stirring constantly. Bring to the boil again. If the jam seems very stiff, add no more than ½ cup of water. Boil for 1 minute, or until the jam sheets off the spoon. Pour into hot, sterilized jars. Cover with new, clean, hot caps. (See section in introduction on jar and cover preparation, pages 24–25.) Invert for 5 minutes.

Makes 7–8 eight-ounce jars

When Locusts Sing It's Cherry-Picking Time

August explodes on Cape Cod. The air becomes heavy; the heat simmers up in waves before your eyes; the birds sing only in the very early morning, and the beach grass, brilliantly green in July, changes ever so subtly, the slightest tinges of gold tipping the edges of the blades. It is then that I start listening for the song of the locust. As much a temperature gauge as a mating ritual, the earlier in the day I hear its high-pitched, ratcheting song, the hotter I know it will be. As the days go by, the song becomes more insistent, more frantic. "Find me, find me," it seems to scream. It is then that I know it's time to find *me* some cherries!

Wild cherries, sometimes called chokecherries, like to grow where forests have previously grown, where roads have been cut and where there is plenty of sun. When the trees bloom, clouds upon clouds of small white flowers cover the branches. Ah, I say to myself, it's going to be a good year.

When I was a child my father would collect wild cherries, put a couple of quarts in a jar, add sugar and put the jar in a dark place. In due time, it fermented and became "bellyache medicine." One tablespoon was supposed to cure all stomach symptoms, including diarrhea. I've absolutely no doubt that most of my bouts with some mysterious malady or other were simply my desire to taste, once more, that wonderful bittersweet, hot in-the-throat liquid. And if it "cured" me, so much the better!

Now, I put on my long pants, gather my small buckets, my ten-quart tub, the bug spray, call the dog and set off. I have a spot. I found it roaming around years ago. I have my favorite elderberry spot, my beach plum spots, know where the best wild blueberries and huckleberries grow. And my wild cherry tree spot.

As I drive down the long-since-abandoned railbed, I peer eagerly upwards, looking for the cherries. It's not until I get into the sunshine that I spot what I've come for. On each side of the road, as far as I can see, are the trees, some as small as six feet high, others older and much taller, dripping with cherries. Bent down, each branch is covered with pea-sized, dark, regal purple-blue fruit. I can actually feel my pulse quicken as my body responds to some deeply buried, age-old imperative. I will have fruit. Quickly, I pull my car off the road, spray my arms and head to keep the green head flies away and set out. Never mind the heat. Never mind the bugs. Never mind having to wade through poison ivy. I will have fruit. Never mind sweat dripping into my eyes, stinging so I can hardly see. I will have fruit. Stretching and bending, I'm aware, as I pick, of the silence. Only the birds chirp as they hurry from one tree to another, storing up fat for their long southern trip. On the ground, I see rabbit and deer droppings, as these animals, too, come to browse. And I think about my intrusion—my invasion, with my car, of this pristine, quiet place; my footsteps, my rustling through branches. I feel my breath slow down as the rhythm of picking, filling buckets and going from tree to tree continues. Sometimes I'm aware that it's not sweat that's dripping from my eyes, but tears, remembering the last time Len and I picked together. Partially paralyzed from bone cancer, he came lurching down the road on unsteady, resistant legs. With his six feet four inches, he could reach the highest branches. How he struggled to stay involved with life, my life. I can still see him reluctantly going to the car to sit, after only a few minutes, exhaustion etched on his face, waiting for me to finish.

I can't reach the highest branches. Like the rest of my life, I am learning to settle for the lower branches, to savor small things, to relish whatever each tree of my life brings me.

If the picking is good, I'll stay until the trees are well picked. I know that I become possessive about getting as much as I possibly can. Perhaps it's because the season is so short, or perhaps I'm responding to some deep-seated urge to make sure I "have enough," whatever that means. In any case, by the time I'm ready to leave, I'm hot, tired and not so sure I ever want to see another cherry.

When I get home, I simply remove as many leaves as possible, pour the berries into gallon-sized bags and pop them in the freezer. When I'm ready, I pour the cherries into a sink filled with cold water. The frozen cherries and leaves float to the surface, and are easier to clean. I put the cherries in a pot, just cover with water and cook slowly until the cherries are soft, generally about 10 minutes. I then put them through the Foley Food Mill, use 1 quart of the juicy puree and freeze the rest. The resulting jam is a deep claret color, deeper than a ruby. Like royal velvet, the jars glow when the light shines through them.

Wild Cherry Jam

4 cups cherry pulp and juice
2 tablespoons lemon juice
1 ½ packages powdered pectin
7 cups sugar

Put the cherry pulp and lemon juice in a large nonreactive pot. Bring to a boil. Add the pectin. Return to the boil. Add the sugar slowly, stirring constantly. Bring to the boil again and boil for 1 minute, or until the jam sheets off the spoon. Pour into hot, sterilized jars. Cover with new, clean, hot caps. (See section in introduction on jar and cover preparation, pages 24–25.) Invert for 5 minutes.

Makes 7–8 eight-ounce jars

Wild Cherry Cordial

Cordial can be described as a somewhat sweet after-dinner liqueur. You generally serve it in little glasses, as it's usually quite potent. I use vodka when I make cordial because it has no taste of its own. The taste of the cherries comes through. This cordial will last for years. I have some that dates back five years. It's now vintage cordial. The taste is better than when I made it. I've even bought beautiful bottles, filled them with cordial and have an instant present when I go visiting.

7–8 cups ripe cherries
3 cups sugar
750 milliliters vodka

Put the cherries in a gallon jar. Add the sugar and the vodka. Punch a few holes in the jar cover. This will allow gases to escape as the cherries ferment. Place the jar in a cool, dark place. Shake carefully every few days for 6 or 7 weeks. Decant the liquid, discarding the cherries.

Makes approximately 2 quarts

This cordial will last indefinitely, tastes wonderful on a cold winter's night when you are snug up against the woodstove, or when you've come in from shoveling out yet again. I sometimes use $^1/_3$ cup of cordial in cherry jam, adding it at the last moment, and bring the jam back to the boil for just a moment. The cordial gives the jam a wonderful added tang.

Breads, Muffins and Other Delectables

In the Beginning

UNTIL I WAS ABOUT TEN YEARS OLD we had an icebox. It was loaded up with ice from the back porch and opened both from the porch and from inside the house, in the pantry. All my friends had refrigerators. I didn't know we weren't very affluent. The icebox was very small, requiring frequent deliveries from the milk, egg, meat, chicken, fish, vegetable and fruit vendors. Everyone delivered.

The drip pan in the lower section of the icebox had to be emptied very frequently, particularly in the summer. My mother hated it.

One day a used electric refrigerator arrived, a gift from Uncle Carl. It was a red-letter day, tinged with a little sadness, for no longer would I be able to jump up on the back of the horse-drawn ice wagon to beg for a chunk of ice from the iceman. My mother was elated. She scrubbed that refrigerator weekly.

I was equally excited when my mother got an electric mixer. It sat on the counter in the pantry, the room adjacent to the kitchen where most of the food preparation and all the dish washing were done. I used to stand on a small stool right next to the counter watching her bake, my nose just inches away from the whirling beaters. I learned well. I also learned from Mr. Myers, the doughnut man. You could smell Mr. Myers before you saw him coming down the walk. He carried a large wicker basket covered with a pristine, white linen napkin. Peeling back the napkin revealed warm, crusty brown hand-cut doughnuts. I learned what homemade meant.

I can't tell you if my mother was an extraordinary baker. I certainly thought she was. I am sure I learned a lot about the steps involved in making cookies, cakes and all sorts of treats.

I've organized the recipes in this section into muffins, quick coffee cakes and breads. All are easy to make. None are too sweet. None use yeast, so they do not take a long time to make.

I use "Texas-sized" muffin pans, which make 6 muffins per batch instead of the usual 12. I spray nonstick pans with a vegetable spray, and also spray the top surface of the pan. This prevents overflowing muffin batter from sticking to the pan, which makes it harder to get the muffins out. I've found that a large flat spoon, run around the edge of each muffin cup, helps release the muffin. There's nothing more discouraging than getting only half a muffin out of the pan!

Bran Muffins

Bran muffins have a nutty, sweet flavor and a slightly firm texture.
I like them with Apple Orange Breakfast Spread (see page 83).

3 eggs
2 cups brown sugar
1½ cups corn oil
4 cups all-bran cereal
4 cups all-purpose flour
4 cups milk
4 teaspoons baking powder
4 teaspoons baking soda
1 cup raisins

In a large bowl, mix all the ingredients by hand or with an electric mixer. Then store in the refrigerator for 24 hours before baking. Use enough batter to fill greased muffin tins three-quarters full. Bake in a preheated 400°F oven for about 20 minutes, or until firm to the touch. Do not overbake.

Makes 60 "Texas-sized" muffins

The batter will keep for up to 1 month in the refrigerator.

The muffins freeze very well and can be reheated in a microwave oven on high, for 1 minute.

Morning Glory Muffins

I first tasted these muffins at the farmers' market. Lisa sold muffins and coffee as well as clams and lobsters. I was an instant convert. Now, I make dozens of them to sell at the church Sea Captains' Fair. There are never any left over. I like them either plain or just with butter. If you can't bear to eat a muffin without jam, try peach. Peach won't overwhelm the delicate flavor of these muffins.

1 cup canola oil
3 eggs, beaten
2 cups grated carrots
1 grated apple
½ cup raisins
½ cup chopped walnuts
½ cup shredded coconut
1 eight-ounce can crushed pineapple, including juice
1 teaspoon vanilla extract
2¼ cups all-purpose flour
1¼ cups sugar
1 tablespoon ground cinnamon
2 teaspoons baking soda

In a large bowl, mix the oil, eggs, carrots, apple, raisins, nuts, coconut, pineapple and vanilla. In a separate bowl, mix the remaining ingredients. Combine and spoon into greased muffin tins. Bake at 400°F in a preheated oven for 20 minutes.

Makes 18 "Texas-sized" muffins or 36 regular-sized ones

Lemon Ginger Muffins

This may sound like an unusual combination for muffins. The ginger adds a nice bite. They taste good with Five-Fruit Marmalade (see page 92).

2 cups all-purpose flour
½ teaspoon baking soda
1 teaspoon baking powder
¼ teaspoon salt
½ cup softened butter
⅔ cup sugar
4 teaspoons chopped preserved ginger
2 eggs, beaten lightly
1 cup milk
½ teaspoon lemon oil

Sift together flour, baking soda, baking powder and salt. Set aside. Cream softened butter and sugar with an electric mixer until light and fluffy. Add ginger and eggs; beat until blended and volume doubles.

Alternately stir milk and flour into mixture, beginning and ending with milk. Stir in lemon oil.

Fill greased muffin tins three-quarters full. Bake at 325°F in a preheated oven until golden brown, for 20–25 minutes.

Makes 12 regular or 6 large muffins

Cranberry Orange Muffins

Marty Andersen not only told us where to find blueberries, he gave me his recipe for cranberry orange muffins. I'm sure that it's the same recipe you can find in any cookbook. It's special for me. Marty Andersen was a special person in my life. These muffins go well with any kind of marmalade.

⅓ cup fresh or dried* cranberries (I like to use dried)
⅓ cup plus 2 tablespoons sugar
3 tablespoons boiling water
2 cups all-purpose flour
2½ teaspoons baking powder
½ teaspoon baking soda
½ teaspoon salt
2 eggs
1 cup milk
⅓ cup melted butter
1 tablespoon grated orange peel

In a small bowl, stir together the cranberries and 2 tablespoons of sugar. Stir in boiling water; set aside for 15 minutes to soften cranberries.

In a large bowl, mix the flour, ⅓ cup of sugar, baking powder, baking soda and salt.

In another bowl, beat the eggs lightly.

*Dried cranberries are readily available in most supermarkets or specialty food shops.

Add the milk and melted butter and beat until smooth. Stir in cranberries with liquid and grated orange peel. Stir liquid mixture into flour mixture.

Spoon into greased muffin cups three-quarters full.

Bake in a preheated 400°F oven for 15–20 minutes, until the muffins are a golden brown.

Makes 12 regular or 6 large muffins

Apricot Pecan Muffins

Recently, I've discovered orange and lemon oil, and use them in all kinds of recipes. And what better jam to use with apricot muffins than apricot jam?

2 cups all-purpose flour
1 teaspoon salt
3 teaspoons baking powder
⅓ cup apricot jam
¾ cup milk
2 large eggs, beaten
¼ cup melted butter
⅛ teaspoon orange oil
½ cup finely chopped pecans

In a bowl, sift together the flour, salt and baking powder. In a saucepan, warm the jam until it is dissolved. Remove from heat and mix in the milk and beaten eggs. Combine with the melted butter, dry ingredients and orange oil, and mix until smooth. Stir in the pecans.

Spoon into greased muffin tins three-quarters full.

Bake in a preheated 400°F oven for about 20 minutes, or until the muffins are golden brown.

Makes 6 large muffins

Blueberry Muffins

I always have either some fresh or frozen blueberries in the house during the summer. Blueberries make plain coffee cake special; pancakes regal; and of course, make the best muffins.

2 cups all-purpose flour
¾ teaspoon salt
¼ cup sugar
2 teaspoons baking powder
1 teaspoon ground cinnamon
1 teaspoon grated orange peel
2 eggs
¼ cup melted butter
¾ cup milk
1 cup fresh or frozen unsweetened blueberries

Sift all the dry ingredients together. In a separate bowl, beat the eggs; add the melted butter and milk. Mix the wet ingredients into the dry, stirring quickly. Add the blueberries.

Spoon into greased muffin tins three-quarters full.

Bake in a preheated 400°F oven for 20 minutes, until the muffins are golden brown.

Makes 6 "Texas-sized" or 12 regular size muffins

This is a basic muffin recipe. You can change or enhance this recipe by using apples, figs, walnuts, maple syrup, pecans, etc. A nice addition is dry buttermilk solids: ¼ cup of dry buttermilk powder added to 1 cup of water is equal to 1 cup of liquid milk.

Just add to the dry ingredients, and use warm water instead of milk when mixing the liquid ingredients. The buttermilk makes muffins light and adds a delicate flavor. Dried buttermilk can be found in health food stores and some supermarkets.

Amy's Vegan Zucchini Carrot Muffins

Amy came to the farmers' market to sell her muffins, breads and pies. No eggs, no dairy, no cholesterol. Not fat free and not low calorie. Just the most delicious, moist muffins imaginable. Amy sold out almost every week. The rest of the vendors at the market went without breakfast anticipating her arrival. We watched closely as she set up her table and laid out her baskets filled with muffins and breads. Then we ate. My favorite muffin is the zucchini carrot.

It took me all summer to convince Amy that she could divulge her secret recipe. It was worth the wait. Thanks.

3 cups all-purpose flour

4 teaspoons baking powder

1 teaspoon baking soda

1 teaspoon salt

6 tablespoons cornstarch

¼ teaspoon ground nutmeg

¼ teaspoon ground ginger

2 cups sugar

1 cup safflower oil

6 tablespoons plain rice milk*

2 heaping teaspoons grated lemon peel

1 teaspoon lemon extract

2 teaspoons vanilla extract

2 cups grated zucchini

1 cup grated carrots

*Rice milk can be found in all health food stores and some supermarkets.

In a large bowl, mix together and set aside the flour, baking powder, baking soda, salt, cornstarch, nutmeg and ginger. In another large bowl, combine the sugar, oil, rice milk, lemon peel and extract, and vanilla.

Mix dry ingredients into wet ingredients, alternating with a mixture of the zucchini and carrots. Spoon into greased muffin tins three-quarters full or two 8 × 3¾ × 2½-inch loaf pans.

Bake in a preheated oven at 350°F, for about 30 minutes for muffins, longer for loaves.

Makes 2 loaves, or 12 large muffins

Amy says they are very good with ginger peach jam. I eat them plain.

Zucchini Bread

When the garden produces more zucchinis than you could possibly use and your friends tell you not to leave any more on their doorstep, then it's time to make zucchini bread. Moist and sweet, zucchini bread sliced thin and spread with Pear with Ginger Jam (see page 121) is a tasty treat.

2 cups all-purpose flour
¾ teaspoon baking powder
¾ teaspoon baking soda
¾ teaspoon salt
¾ teaspoon ground cinnamon
3 eggs
1 cup sugar
⅔ cup canola oil
¾ teaspoon lemon extract
1⅓ cups grated unpeeled zucchini
⅔ cup chopped walnuts
⅔ cup raisins

Sift together the flour, baking powder, baking soda, salt and cinnamon. Set aside. Beat eggs with sugar for 2 minutes. Gradually add oil and beat another 2 minutes. Add extract.

Alternately fold in flour mixture and zucchini until evenly moistened. Stir in nuts and raisins. Do not overmix. Pour into a well-greased 9 × 5 × 3-inch pan. Bake in a preheated 350°F oven for about 1¼ hours, until bread tests done. Cool before removing from pan.

Makes 1 small loaf

Irish Soda Bread

The cook in an Irish kitchen must always remember to stir ingredients clockwise—to humor the Druids. When an Irish cook bakes Irish soda bread, she will always cut a cross on the top with a knife before baking to let the Devil out! Rich with butter and currants, Irish soda bread warm from the oven spread with Apple Orange Breakfast Spread (see page 83) needs no incantations to the spirit world. It's magic all its own.

2 cups all-purpose flour
1 teaspoon baking soda
1 teaspoon baking powder
½ teaspoon salt
1 tablespoon sugar
6 tablespoons butter
½ cup dried currants or raisins
¾ cup buttermilk (or 3 tablespoons dry buttermilk and
¾ cup warm water)

Sift the flour, baking soda, baking powder, salt, sugar and butter into the bowl of your food processor. Using short on/off pulses and your cutting blade, process until the mixture looks like cornmeal. This will take only a few seconds. Remove from processor. Add the fruit and most of the buttermilk, beating quickly with a spoon. Mix until a ball is formed, adding more buttermilk a spoonful at a time as needed. Put the dough on a lightly floured surface and pat into a rounded loaf. Put the loaf in a greased 8-inch round baking pan, and bake in a preheated 375°F oven for 40 minutes.

Makes one 8-inch round loaf

Pumpkin Bread

I always buy several small pumpkins instead of one big one at Halloween, anticipating the day when I can take the pumpkins in, open them, roast the seeds, cook the pumpkins and make pumpkin bread. You can also use canned solid pack pumpkin. Since pumpkin bread has a subtle flavor, I like it with plain Strawberry Jam (see page 103). Generally, I use whatever jam is left over after I pour whatever jam I'm making. I save the leftovers and always have samples to use. My bed-and-breakfast guests get to try all kinds of jams this way.

3 cups sugar
3 ½ cups all-purpose flour
1 teaspoon baking powder
2 teaspoons baking soda
½ teaspoon ground cloves
1 teaspoon ground nutmeg
1 teaspoon ground allspice
1 cup canola oil
4 eggs, beaten
1 5-ounce can solid pack pumpkin
½ cup chopped walnuts
⅔ cup water

Sift all the dry ingredients and set aside. Mix the oil, eggs and pumpkin. Add the nuts. Add the flour, alternating with the water. Pour into two greased 8 × 4 × 3-inch pans. Bake in a preheated 350°F oven for 40 minutes, or until nicely brown.

Makes 2 medium-sized loaves

Banana Bread

When Alex, my second-oldest son, was a teenager, he worked for Mr. Houghton at the South Wellfleet General Store. Mr. Houghton let him take all the overripe bananas home for me. I was baking bread for a health food store at the time. Those bananas never went to waste!

2 cups all-purpose flour
2 1/4 teaspoons baking powder
1/2 teaspoon salt
4 tablespoons melted butter
1 cup sugar
3 ripe bananas, mashed
2 eggs, beaten
3/4 teaspoon grated lemon peel
1/2 cup chopped walnuts

Sift and mix the flour, baking powder and salt. Set aside. Beat the butter and sugar until creamy. Mix in the bananas, eggs and lemon peel. Add the nuts. Add the dry ingredients in three parts, mixing well after each addition. Pour into two medium greased bread pans or one large pan. Bake in a preheated 350°F oven for about 1 hour.

Makes *1 large 9 × 5 × 3-inch loaf*

Cranberry Orange Nut Bread

This recipe is similar to the one for Cranberry Orange Muffins (see page 174). Sometimes it's nice to be able to slice bread, spread on cream cheese, make a sandwich and take it to the beach for a long walk. A cranberry orange nut sandwich will taste mighty good when you stop your beachcombing to lean up against the base of a cliff to watch the waves crashing in. Food for the body and the soul.

3 cups all-purpose flour
3 teaspoons baking powder
1/2 cup sugar
1 tablespoon grated orange peel
2 tablespoons canola oil
1 egg
1/4 cup orange juice
1 1/4 cups milk
1/2 cup chopped walnuts
1/2 cup dried* or chopped fresh cranberries

Sift the flour and baking powder. Add the sugar and orange peel and set aside. Combine and beat the oil, egg, orange juice and milk. Add the dry ingredients to the wet, mixing only to moisten. Do not overmix. Add the nuts. Fold the cranberries into the batter. Pour into two 8 × 4 × 3-inch greased baking pans. Bake in a preheated 350°F oven for about 50 minutes.

Makes 2 small loaves

This bread slices easier on the second day.

Dried cranberries are available in most markets or specialty food shops.

Buttermilk Corn Bread

Corn bread tastes best when warm, right out of the oven. Because it's so easy to make, you can do this as a last-minute bread. It's yummy with marmalade and perfect with four-alarm chili. Sometimes I pour the dough on top of a vegetarian casserole. The result is a crusty, juicy meal.

1 cup cornmeal
1 cup all-purpose flour
2 teaspoons baking powder
½ teaspoon baking soda
3 tablespoons sugar
1 egg, beaten
¼ cup corn oil
1 cup buttermilk (or 4 tablespoons dry buttermilk and
    1 cup warm water)
Ground nutmeg or chopped preserved ginger (optional)

Mix the dry ingredients. Stir in the egg, oil and buttermilk. Pour into a greased 9-inch square pan. Bake in a preheated 425°F oven for 25 minutes. Do not overbake.

Makes one 9-inch square pan

Corn bread should be moist. I like to add a little nutmeg or a little chopped preserved ginger.

To make a vegetarian casserole: put sautéed onions, mushrooms, green peppers, broccoli, carrots, summer squash and cauliflower into a casserole, pour cornbread mix on top and bake at 350°F for 40 minutes.

Quick Coffee Cake

This coffee cake is a staple in my repertoire. You can add blueberries, diced apples, chopped dried apricots; enhance it with different flavorings—it's a forgiving cake.

1 ¼ cups all-purpose flour
2 teaspoons baking powder
½ teaspoon salt
⅓ cup soft butter or vegetable shortening
¾ cup sugar
1 egg
1 teaspoon vanilla or almond extract
⅔ cup milk

STREUSEL TOPPING

3 tablespoons all-purpose flour
3 tablespoons softened butter
5 tablespoons brown sugar

Sift the flour, baking powder and salt and set aside. Beat the butter and sugar until creamy. Add the egg and vanilla. Mix in the dry ingredients, alternating with the milk. Pour half the batter into a greased 8-inch round or 9-inch square pan.

Mix the topping ingredients until crumbly. You can add cinnamon, nutmeg, coconut, chopped nuts, etc.

Sprinkle in half the streusel topping. Pour in the rest of the cake batter. Sprinkle on the rest of the streusel topping. Bake in a preheated 375°F oven for about 25 minutes.

Makes one 8-inch round or 9-inch square pan

Bread Pudding

As the winter winds begin to blow, the clock gets turned back and night swoops down earlier and earlier. Frosty early-morning walks become crunchy underfoot. My bed-and-breakfast guests appreciate a nontraditional breakfast—individual bread puddings baked in pretty ramekins, topped with bubbling cranberry applesauce.

5 cups diced bread crumbs (I use Portuguese sweet bread)
3 cups warm milk
3 eggs
½ cup sugar
1 teaspoon vanilla extract
1 teaspoon grated orange peel
½ cup raisins

Soak the bread in the milk for 20 minutes. Add the remaining ingredients and pour into a buttered baking dish set in a pan of hot water. Bake in a preheated 350°F oven for 45 minutes. Serve hot in small dishes or spoon into individual ramekins and top with cranberry applesauce. Place under the broiler and broil until the sauce bubbles. Serve hot. Yummy!

Makes one 9 × 13-inch pan

Date Nut Loaf

This recipe is older than I am. I remember my mother soaking dates to put into this date nut bread. It's been a favorite of my children. Flavor cream cheese with a tiny bit of rum. Spread on slices of date nut bread. Have company for tea. Elegant.

1 teaspoon baking soda
1 cup chopped dates
¾ cup boiling water
2 eggs
¾ cup sugar
1¾ cups all-purpose flour
½ cup chopped walnuts
2 tablespoons melted butter
1 teaspoon vanilla extract

Sprinkle baking soda over the chopped dates. Pour boiling water over the dates. Let stand until cool. Beat the eggs and sugar until fluffy. Drain off the water from the dates and add it to the egg mixture. Add sifted flour, dates and walnuts. Add melted butter and vanilla. Pour into a well-greased 9 × 5 × 3-inch pan. Bake in a preheated oven at 350°F for 45 minutes.

Makes one 9 × 5 × 3-inch loaf

Pineapple Nut Bread

This bread is a bit sweeter than most. Since it tends to be moist, I let it sit for a day or two before slicing. It also freezes well. It's particularly good toasted, with Cranberry Lime Jam (see page 44).

1½ cups all-purpose flour
3 teaspoons baking powder
1 teaspoon salt
⅓ cup sugar
2 eggs, beaten
⅔ cup pineapple juice
1 cup canned crushed pineapple, drained
1½ cups uncooked oats (quick cooking)
⅔ cup chopped walnuts
½ cup melted butter

Sift together the dry ingredients. Combine the eggs and pineapple juice. Add to the dry ingredients, mixing only until the dry ingredients are dampened. Fold in the pineapple, oats, nuts and butter. Pour into a well-greased 9 × 5 × 3-inch pan. Bake in a preheated 350°F oven for 1¼ hours.

Makes one 9 × 5 × 3-inch loaf

Dried Cranberry Scones

I'll be the first to admit that my initial attempts to make light, tender scones were not rousing successes. The first few batches ended up out in the yard, where the crows gobbled them up. I didn't give up. The crows continued to eat well. Finally I figured out the trick. You have to be very gentle when mixing scones. A very light touch with the mixing spoon is all you need. Scones are not bread. They can't be beaten. This recipe was tried out by my daughter, who called to tell me that her family liked them. I've also tried them out. They are really special.

½ cup plus 2 tablespoons buttermilk (I use powdered
    buttermilk that can be reconstituted)
1 large egg
1 teaspoon vanilla extract
5 tablespoons sugar
2¼ cups regular cake flour (not self-rising)
½ teaspoon salt
1 tablespoon baking powder
½ teaspoon baking soda
6 tablespoons cold butter, cut into bits
½ cup dried cranberries*
¼ cup preserved or crystallized minced ginger

In a bowl, whisk together ½ cup of the buttermilk, the egg, vanilla and 3 tablespoons of the sugar. In another bowl, mix together the flour, salt, baking powder and baking soda. Blend in

*Available in most markets or specialty food shops.

the butter until the mixture looks like cornmeal. Stir in the cranberries, the ginger and the buttermilk mixture with a fork until the dough just clings together. It will be sticky. Gently knead the dough for no more than 30 seconds. Pat the dough into a ¾-inch-thick round, place in a greased 8-inch round pan and score into wedges. Brush with the remaining buttermilk. Sprinkle with 2 tablespoons sugar. Bake in a preheated oven at 400°F for about 15 minutes, or until golden.

Makes 8 scones

Sesame Orange Scones

These scones go very well with quiche. Instead of making one large quiche, I bake individual ones in little tart pans I found at my local cook shop. Each guest is guaranteed a nice hot breakfast. I have to admit that these scones really don't need any jam. If you are a marmalade addict, however, try Ginger Peach Marmalade (see page 119). It's a nice combination of sweet and tangy.

½ cup toasted sesame seeds
3 tablespoons grated orange rind
3 cups all-purpose flour
3 tablespoons light brown sugar
1 tablespoon baking powder
¾ teaspoon salt
¾ cup vegetable shortening
1 cup orange juice
3 tablespoons granulated sugar

Grease a cookie sheet. Set aside 1 tablespoon of the sesame seeds and 1 teaspoon of the orange rind. In a large bowl, combine the flour, the remaining sesame seeds and orange rind, the brown sugar, baking powder and salt. With a pastry blender or two knives, cut in the shortening until the mixture looks like cornmeal. Reserve 1 tablespoon of orange juice. Add the remaining orange juice to the dry ingredient mixture. Mix lightly with a fork until the batter clings together and forms a soft dough. Knead gently on a floured surface just a few times. With floured hands, pat into a 7-inch round. Cut into four wedges.

Place scones 1 inch apart on the greased baking sheet. Pierce the tops with the tines of a fork. Heat the remaining orange juice and the granulated sugar until they boil; stir in remaining orange peel and brush the tops of the scones. Sprinkle with the remaining sesame seeds. Bake in a preheated 425°F oven for 15 minutes, or until golden brown. Brush again with the orange glaze. Serve warm.

Makes 4 scones

Epilogue

The Hawk

THE FIRST TIME THE HAWK came to the yard we sat, we two, looking at each other, sizing each other up. It was my first full day in my new house. He (I'm sure it is a "he") sat on a tree limb, not five feet from the edge of the deck.

I was not where I belonged. This was not *my* turf. This was not where *my* memories lay in wait. This place was a void. No memories. Who would be a part of my memories? Who would share this space with me? Do you have to have ecstasy and pain to have memories? Do you have to have losses and rebirth to have memories? How would I create memories at this stage in my life? I was afraid that this place would be just a house and not a home. How will I make it a warm loving home . . . all alone. It is easier when you can bless your house with great love. It is easier when you have resolved conflicts and shared the space. It is hard to "live" in an empty house. Oh, I knew it was not empty in the truest sense. All my "things" were here. But it was empty. The house had no soul. I would have to work very hard to create a soul in this house.

How wonderful, I thought. I'm not alone. He stayed for several minutes, finally drifting silently away through the tree-tops.

The next day he was back. And the next. And the next. For

almost a week that hawk watched me from the same tree limb. One day I spotted him on the deck eating a toad.

It was then I realized the hawk was Len, come to watch me as I settled in—me, who thought he would never find me once I had moved. He had come to observe: to see if I was doing well; to let me know that I was not alone. I wanted to screech at him; to tell him that I didn't want to be here; that I hadn't wanted to scatter his ashes over the marsh; that I wanted to grow old with him in that other wonderful place; that I didn't want to be rattling around all alone in this alien place. The hawk just observed, silently winging away when he had checked me out. I missed him when a day went by and he didn't come.

The first Mother's Day in my new house came. A daughter was visiting. The hawk landed on the deck, right outside the sliding glass doors. He stayed for several minutes. "Look," she said. "Dad's come for a visit."

"You too?" I was dumbfounded. I wasn't the only one who felt that presence. Hardly a week went by without the hawk making an appearance.

One day there were two hawks circling the house calling. "How come," I yelled up, "how come you've found someone and I've not?"

One bright summer day three hawks circled and called. A family!

Another Mother's Day came. The house had absorbed laughter and tears, music and smells. Jam pots crowded the stove; fruit for jam making filled the freezers. Children and grandchildren have run up and down, in and out. Birds feed at the feeders and bathe in the birdbaths. Flowers bloom in riotous abundance. Peach, pear and apricot trees bloom. Beach sand filters in. Seashells collect on the deck. Towels and bathing suits drape over the railings. Vegetables grow and get harvested. More and more jam gets made. The house had grown a soul. I had discovered mine.

The hawk came down and sat on the deck. My Mother's Day present once again.

I could smile.

One day, down at the pond, a neighbor said, "Look. There's a hawk circling your house and calling."

"That's just my husband, come to check me out."

Come again and again. Watch me. My heart soars with you. My feet are firmly on the ground.

Appendix

THE FOLLOWING IS A LIST of mail-order sources for some of the ingredients used in jam making. Fruit should be bought locally if at all possible, to reduce the chance of spoilage as well as to keep down transportation costs.

BROOKSTONE
5 VOSE FARM ROAD
PETERBOROUGH, NH 03458
603-924-7181

I first used Brookstone as a source of hard-to-find unique tools. Now, Homewares carries the same quality line of shelving, storage containers, office organizing supplies, etc.

CAPE BOTTLE
P.O. BOX 1717
MANOMET, MA 12345
508-833-6307
TEL./FAX 508-833-6305

These people ship jars, canisters and imported bottles of all kinds all over. They're accommodating, friendly and interested in anyone who's starting out.

CHEF'S CATALOGUE
3915 COMMERCIAL AVENUE

NORTHBROOK, IL 60062
312-480-9400

When this catalog has a sale, stock up! They carry all the best-known names of kitchen equipment, as well as some hard-to-find specialty items.

CONCORD FOODS
10 MINUTEMAN WAY
BROCKTON, MA 02401
508-580-1700

I get my preserved ginger from this supplier. They also carry all kinds of ingredients for candy making.

GARDENER'S SUPPLY COMPANY
133 ELM STREET
WINOOSKI, VT 05054
802-655-9006

From planting kits to canning pots. I've visited these folks. Nice, helpful people.

PACIFIC PECTIN
40179 ENTERPRISE DRIVE BOULEVARD,
    7BD
OAKHURST, CA 93644
209-683-0303

These people make pectin from lemon and lime peels. They sell it in 50- or 100-pound boxes. I know that sounds like a lot. Fifty pounds will make 2,500 jars. If you get ten friends together, you can each have 5 pounds—enough pectin for all of your jam making. I keep the pectin well covered, just taking out 5 pounds at a time, storing it in a stainless steel canister. It is much cheaper than buying it at the market and will keep indefinitely.

RYKOFF SEXTON
140 MORGAN DRIVE
NORWOOD, MA 02062
617-762-9200

Although these people are New England based, they ship all over the country, everything from soup to nuts, frozen foods, cleaning equipment—anything and everything you could possibly need.

WILLIAMS-SONOMA
P.O. BOX 7456
SAN FRANCISCO, CA 94120-7456
415-652-1515

This is the source of Ma Made Marmalade Mix. You can get thick or thin sliced orange marmalade mix or lemon marmalade mix. Williams-Sonoma has outlets in cities all across the country, which might be a less expensive way of getting what you need. They carry excellent-quality kitchen tools, gourmet foods, orange and lemon oils, etc. I look forward to getting the catalog.

ZABAR'S
2245 BROADWAY
NEW YORK, NY 10024
212-787-2000

Upstairs at Zabar's is the biggest assortment of cooking utensils, pots, bowls, etc., that I've ever seen. Downstairs are all kinds of the most exotic foods imaginable, including the busiest takeout counter around. It's truly one place to visit in New York. You'll never see anything like it anywhere else.

Index